ANOTHER SET OF
LENSES

Exploring our **perceptions and paradigms** and how they shape our story

Steve Hall

First published by Steve Hall, 2021

Copyright © 2021 Steve Hall

www.stevehall.co.za

978-1-928539-93-3   (Paperback)

978-1-928539-92-6   (ebook)

Cover Design and Typesetting by www.myebook.online

ENDORSEMENTS

"Steve has become a close friend of our company's. He has added tremendous value in all his interventions with us. The material and the content has always been superb, but the way Steve delivers it makes it come alive in our people and in our organisation. He has a very special way of engaging and communicating and my team always looks forward to spending time with him."

Sean Robinson, Joint MD Ulta Liquors

"Steve's insights into how to mobilize human energy in driving transformational performance is truly unique."

Mark Sardi, Group CEO Ascendis

"Steve has expertly guided our Partner team at IQbusiness on our leadership path over the past 3 years - not that we are slow on the take up, but because Steve keeps facilitating ways to expand our horizon, boost our energy and rise to the challenge as we continue to grow."

Adam Craker, CEO IQ Business

"Steve is incomparable in how he is able to make his ideas so accessible to everyone. His insights are so real, so human and so wise. What a legend!"

Adele Ungaretti, Executive Leadership Development The Standard Bank Group

TABLE OF CONTENTS

INTRODUCTION

P.S.

Wait a moment…

You might be asking whether the editor has made an error, or whether you have the book back to front. By definition, a P.S. must surely come at the end?

Fear not, for everything has a reason; besides, in some strange way, you might already have read this book. The stories you will read here may well be your stories, and at the very least, you will have lived some of the lessons which these stories could serve to inspire.

So please, read on.

A postscript (P.S.) is an afterthought, thought of occurring after the letter has been written and signed. The term comes from the Latin postscriptum, an expression meaning "written after" (which may be interpreted in the sense of "that which comes after the writing").

Wikipedia

Anyone who has ever played golf knows about an ancient Chinese philosophy; a second ball is placed with resignation on the tee some deep-breathing and vein-popping moments after the first ball has been sent slicing out of bounds, or slapped without its teeth in tact towards a watery grave. With muscles a bit more relaxed, and no sense of expectation, the second ball finds flight down the middle of the fairway, or grips and holds true on the oasis of green. Perhaps resignation is the word worth repeating here, as there may be a sense of effortless surrender to the outcome. The ego is still attached to the first projectile, and it— along with the ball—is unrecoverable. It is out of sight.

At this point there is normally someone in the covey who pipes up:

"Ancient Chinese philosophy...Hit second ball first."

And so, I write my second book first.

I have written stories, essays, and anecdotes, and even some poetry for a number of decades. Every now and then, I'd share my work with a few for whom they might have been relevant; but mostly, they've been filed into folders, jammed into journals, or stored as soft copies.

The fear of the piercing light of vulnerability have kept them well hidden from view and well preserved by their neighbouring thoughts as the dragons of doubt fight with the gremlins of comparison and peer over the fence of perceived safety. Of course, the most dangerous dragons are not outside the walls of our own making. They spit and snarl and sneeze their sulphurous fumes from within, and their flames are fanned by the fuel from the searing—yet, almost silent—breath of our own internal critics.

We are so often the providers of the very air which fire needs to burn, and we are all too eager to throw another log onto the internal inferno of self-preservation.

As a result, books remain unwritten, stories are left untold, and the ash heaps hold memory whilst the world needs more magic.

A close friend and colleague always reminds me that there is less time than we think, and as I have just reached my fifties, and have raised my bat to five fascinating decades, it is time perhaps to breathe some life into these reflections. I have lived my entire life in the exact same geographical borders of two countries, and I have spent precisely half of my fifty years in each one. How is that possible, you may well ask. How can you have lived in two countries which over that time have the identical physical borders?

Has there been a name change in that land?

Of course, I'm talking about South Africa. For twenty-five years, I lived in the old one, and for twenty-five years, I have lived in the new. This is not a history lesson about the two, but rather a series of thoughts and observations of the one thing which has bridged this remarkable place.

Humanity.

Stories of humanity are timeless and belong to no political dispensation, and so I tee up my second book first; safe in the knowledge that the stories are already written. Perhaps they just need to be shared.

So, please join me around the fire with a cup of coffee—or something different; maybe even a cigar—and enjoy a walk down a fairway of afterthoughts as we connect with some great characters and a few chosen reflections. Perhaps as we sit in the smoke and significance of the stories, we may even reconnect with ourselves.

And, if by any chance, something ignites your imagination, in the true spirit of storytelling around an African fire, please feel free to share it with others. I have never heard of a fireside tale with a copyright attached. Besides, I hope to hear some of your stories someday.

This book starts with a P.S., which is a little back to front. Maybe it is that kind of book. Sometimes a look through a different lens allows us to see a world previously unseen or perhaps temporarily forgotten.

Take a seat around this fire where our shadows are both finitely separate and infinitely connected, and let's share some stories together.

Victor Borge, the Danish-American pianist and comedian once said:

"The shortest distance between two people is a smile."

Many people since then have said that maybe the shortest distance between two people is a story.

You are all welcome, and I hope you are smiling!

Does This Book Have a Story or Is This a Book of Stories?

Yes.

In the world we live in right now, this is an easy answer to a double question. Should we invest in our people, or should we cut costs? Yes. Should we produce a quality service or should we be accessible to a lower income market? Yes. Should I save for an uncertain future, or should I live in the now? Yes. Should I focus on my career or follow my passion? Yes.

These are all questions I have heard as a facilitator of learning for over twenty-five years. I have always felt so wise when I have rolled this infinitely frustrating answer off of its Socratic shelf; and I know it is frustrating, because I received the same response when I asked a young man (who you will read more about later in this book) this leading question.

Should I write a story kind of book, or just a book of stories?

His answer was predictably, "Yes!"

I expected a lot more wisdom, a definite answer, or—at least— some guidance; but as he stared with a knowing smile over his steaming coffee on a Johannesburg suburban street corner, I sensed immediately that I was receiving a dose of my own medicine. Only I can figure out my journey. I was the only architect of the structure and decorator of its interior; only I could write down what has cropped up.

In my journals to my children, I have made reference to a timeless quote from Joseph Campbell, an American Professor of Literature and Mythology:

"If you can see your path laid out in front of you step by step, you know it's not your path. Your own path you make with every step you take. That's why it's your path."

It struck me that dispensing advice and dishing out inspiring quotes is a lot easier than taking them to heart and living their intentions.

Craig Kanyemba, a man less than half my age at the time of writing, adjusted his Covid mask to sip once more from his coffee, and smiled again. He has written six books of his own and self-published them all. He has taken a lot of steps on his own path. In this journey of writing, I was about to take my first, and I had no idea on what substrate that first step would fall.

At the time, I didn't know that each new step would open my eyes to different challenges and awaken some exciting possibilities. By listening, Craig had allowed a seed to be planted; over time, it germinated in the soils of space.

I left that street corner café with a sense of an answer in its ambiguity.

Yes. This would be a book with a story, but also a book of stories.

So, what's the story?

Firstly, this book is not my story, and whilst elements of my life may emerge during the telling, the real message lies in the magic of others. If we stop long enough to truly see another, we may discover more than we could ever have imagined. I'm not sure how often I really paused to learn from the lives of some fellow pathfinders along the way during the first half of my life.

Perhaps I had been more tourist and occasional traveller than a true pilgrim, and the analogy of these (different) ways of living still resonates through the channels of my own choices.

A tourist will follow the guide book and only eat at the recommended restaurants. The concierge of a stable and reliable brand of hotel chain will be their chosen consultant, and no move will be made without a pre-prepared plan for the day. Trips will have been booked and paid for, and receipts will be efficiently filed in the event of a well-earned refund. The weather has been checked and rechecked, and appropriate clothing is packed.

The next three meals are certainties, as are the right seats to enjoy them from, and photos are taken of every conceivable dish and posted on Instagram. My pristine holiday should blend in well with my perfect life, and all the boxes are ticked.

The 'must sees' have been seen with manipulated memories well moulded by Photoshop, and any gifts for the folks back home are bought with time to spare in the duty free stores of certainty.

Been there. Done that. Bought the t-shirt.

I have been that same tourist at times. Craving the safety of the hotel room and not the perceived chaos of the streets. Eating what you know and knowing what you eat. Engaging only in the language of English and never for too long, in case you step into the dark of discomfort.

Stick to the plan and don't stray from the script. Try to predict the future and then take careful and cautious steps to reach it. The pages of the *Lonely Planet* have been written for a reason: just go where others have been before; it is there where you capture the signature shot of popular postcards.

My outlay has matched my objectives and I can claim to have 'done' New York or South America, or The East—as if any of those remarkable places can ever be 'done', even by those who live there.

Though, whenever I come home with real stories to tell and not just photographs to show, it is because I have delved into the mindset of a traveller. I have wandered off the beaten path of a million camera traps, walked past the overpriced queues, and settled into some street food. I have listened for the language of locals to find the real coffee made with love, and a burger created with flair.

I have not been manacled by the chains of convenience of the high street megastores. I have stopped to ask for directions, and in the process started a conversation which I have never had with 'Waze' or 'Google Maps', and I have been beautifully burned by the tricksters in the backstreets.

A traveller wants to become a little lost and enjoys the cut and thrust of a bout of bargaining. They will happily shift their schedule and alter their agenda, open to any number of extraneous factors. Travellers will see life through some different lenses, they will go with the flow and they will follow and feed off the energy along their journey.

More recently, I have meandered the twists and turns of my own Zizyphus branch—the buffalo thorn of the story of my life—and I have found time to 'wait a bit' in reflection at this point of inflection. I have looked back at the hooked thorn of my past and remembered, and I now stare forward along the straight thorn of the future and a new realisation.

There is another way to see this world, and that might be in the way of the pilgrim.

Whilst this term of pilgrim often has a deep religious connection, a more inclusive and modern use seems to lie in the realm of spirituality. A pilgrim appears where their spirit may call them. An artist might go on a pilgrimage to The Louvre in Paris, and a dyed in the wool Liverpool FC fan will save for years to go to Anfield. If you're a golfer, you will want to walk the hallowed turf of St Andrew's in Scotland, and with every footfall, you will leave a piece of your soul on its soil.

Maybe a pilgrim journeys for a greater purpose or a deeper meaning, but at the heart of every pilgrimage lies a sacrifice. You must give something back or offer something up to be on the uncharted road of the pilgrim. Maybe you give support or encouragement. Perhaps you offer empathy or guidance, or even hope, or a smile, or a hopeful smile at the very least. A pilgrim will simply give themselves to the situation with as much compassion as they can muster, along with minimal judgement. They are fully present in that moment.

In general—and without stretching the metaphor too far—tourists and travellers want to gain something from their experience: A photo, a ticked bucket list item, a break, a new angle for our Instagram posts; maybe even inner harmony. A pilgrim's voyage is determined by what we give. A warm greeting, a listening ear, a story, or a simple act of humanity. Pete Laburn, a wise colleague and mentor—and more importantly, a friend—has always questioned:

"Why is anyone the richer for even thirty seconds spent with you?"

That question is the pilgrim's mantra. Their motivation lies in meaning, their gift is their giving and their service is their sacrifice.

We all approach life as a combination of all three, and we needn't move far in physical distance to be on any one of these paths. I can be tourist, traveller, and pilgrim in the same hour, and I can be all three in the confined space of my own home, and even with my own thoughts. As a father, I have demanded compliance from my children like a tourist might expect a refund on a cloudy day when the mountains weren't postcard perfect. I have sought to earn their respect as if I were an entitled authority, and I have angled for affirmation from my own wife.

Occasionally, I have travelled off the beaten path of parenthood with them, and really tried to look at their world through an unadulterated perspective, and in so doing, we have made more progress and had more fun in the exploration as fellow travellers.

All too rarely, I sat down in the spirit of the pilgrim and gave them the sanctity of space and the security of support; but have truly received way more in return. The gratification just isn't often instant, and the reward is never measurable in a linear sense.

I believe that the mindset of a tourist, a traveller, or a pilgrim cuts through all barriers, including economic barriers. It is not where we sit on the plane, or how many stars surround the accommodation we sleep in; what matters more seems to lie in how we journey, who we are, and whose lives are left even a smile richer through our presence.

A tourist might be cautious and values clarity.

A traveller might show courage and enjoys curiosity.

A pilgrim lives in the question and seeks connection.

None of these approaches are wrong. On the contrary, at times we need to follow the guidebooks and stick to the path and take heed when the bus conductor tells us not to step off at the stop in South Central Los Angeles. Great clarity in the instruction—and caution in following it—might save your backpack, or even your life.

But if I keep my head in the App or the map and fail to look up, I will miss the sparkle in the eyes of my children when they see the Eiffel Tower or Big Ben for the first time, and that moment never comes back. The map will still be there if I need it.

For a few treasured months of my life in the mid-1990s, I worked at The Covey Leadership Centre in Provo, Utah in America. It was as steep and exciting a learning curve as I can ever remember and I was fully immersed in the world and the ways of Stephen Covey's *7 Habits of Highly Effective People* and *First Things First*. It formed the basis and the backbone of my life for the next ten years. If there is one model and teaching which has stood out for me since then and forever will, it is *The Basic Change* model summed up by eight letters in three extraordinary words.

SEE-DO-GET.

It is tempting to tear into some teaching or fly into a flurry of facilitation, but this was never really the aim of this book. It is however important to understand the impact and the links of these words in the formation of habits, and to provide some context for this story as it unfolds.

We have pictures in our minds of everything from going to the dentist to a tropical island beach holiday. We have mental mind maps of the work we love and the chores we detest.

We have images of people—real and imagined, individuals and groups. Political parties, sports teams, the staff at our favourite restaurant and corrupt officials, family members, and even taxi drivers.

These pictures can arrive in our minds' eyes in a millisecond. They appear in High Definition with a crystal quality clarity and fuse a focus from the far reaches of our memory banks. These mental constructs have been erected from the building blocks of belief, patterned by the paint of past experience, and most certainly manipulated by the media.

On our *Lead with Humanity* experiences, we often comment that your view of America will depend on whether you watch CNN or Fox News. We will speak a lot about polar opposites in the thoughts and stories ahead. The way we see the world is coloured by our cultures and laced with legacy, and our pictures are reinforced through relationships.

Our behaviours are informed by these pictures, and these paradigms may act as the catalyst of our reactions. We DO what we do because we SEE what we see. If I see an exciting opportunity, I will likely work towards it; and if I see you as a friendly person, there is a significant chance my behaviour will be open, honest, and trustworthy. Similarly, if I see someone as untrustworthy, I won't vote for them; and if I see a company acting unethically, I will buy from someone else.

We **Do** what we do, because we **See** what we see.

When we DO something, we ACHIEVE an outcome; if we ACHIEVE an outcome which reinforces our picture, we form habits. The SEE informs the DO. The DO results in a GET—and if our habits are strong for good or for bad—the GET reaffirms the SEE. It all seems to work incredibly well when we are happy with the outcomes we achieve, but when we feel that our outcomes are sub optimal, that challenges us.

I have spent a large part of my working life in leadership development and team effectiveness, trying hard to effect change by focusing on the DO—the behaviours. Whilst this is of course an important component to address, I am learning that if I want to change my own behaviours, I must understand the underlying pictures which caused the behaviours in the first place.

This is not a book on behaviour change; it is simply a look through different lenses, belonging to some extraordinary people who have crossed my path. Some have shown courage in the full face of fear. Others have given where it seemed as though there was nothing left to give.

You may meet the hopeful few in a sea of hopelessness, and those who smile through their storms. Some of these reflections may mirror some of Humanity's finest who have crossed your paths along your own journey, and if they have, please tell me. I will already be the richer for thirty seconds spent with you.

More importantly, if you meet these Angels with messages of meaning, please tell them of the impact they have had. If you meet yourself in these pages, I hope you will enjoy the company!

Therein lies the story of this book of stories.

"If you change the way you look at things, the things you look at change."

Wayne Dyer

In the next section, we will venture into the world of pictures, including pictures of our world. Each picture and its opposite set of lenses will be illustrated with a handful of stories, and whilst most of them might have occurred in Africa, the continent of my birth, they really belong to all of Humanity.

Some of these stories were written many years ago, and some of them may overlap or at least find meaning in other chapters. To that end, you might read it from start to finish, or you may just open the book in a random place and choose to read a story.

As I mentioned before, there is a story to the book, but it is also a book of stories.

So—whether as a tourist, a traveller, or a pilgrim or a combination of all three, as we all are—please grab a coffee, clean your readers, and walk with me as we wander through some wonderings, or meander through some musings.

But first, let me tell you a story about a personal turning point.

A Personal Turning Point

Since childhood, I have been fascinated by the African analogy behind a remarkable tree called the Zizyphus Mucronata. I remember being enthralled by a Shangaan tracker called Million who could call in a Scops Owlet with his shrill, yet strangely guttural whistle.

During the hot days of the lowveld summer, when parents were escaping the heat, Million would facilitate interpretive walks for the youth. We would explore the small but significant stories of the wild, which are so easily missed in a Big Five drive-by safari. With an old knife and a dramatic pause, this naturalist and story teller would take a cutting of The Buffalo Thorn tree, and explain how it carries great expression and significant meaning in its Afrikaans name, 'Blinkblaar Wag 'n Bietjie' doring boom. 'Blinkblaar' means shiny leaf, and even without any summer rains, the leaves shine as if recently polished and waxed. To me, the gripping part of the story lay in the meaning of the term 'Wag 'n Bietjie' which means to 'wait a bit'.

You only have to be caught in the tangled web of its crooked branches and thorns once to realise that you can't be in a hurry to move on. You simply have to be patient and unpick yourself from its clutches. The 'doring boom' is the thorn tree, and it bears serious thorns.

The multiple branch networks are diagnostically zig zag in structure. The Nguni people of Southern Africa relate these branches to the journey of our lives. It is never a straight road. It is not always a dual carriageway with painted lines and bright reflective cat's eyes to show us the way in the dark. It is not free of potholes, and neither is it lit up with street lights.

The way of our travels is through an ongoing series of twists and turns which occur throughout our lives. Some of these turning points are expected. We learn to ride a bike, we start a new school, we write exams. Maybe we expect to marry our soulmate someday, or to have children, but maybe we won't.

The road ahead carries the unforeseen, too, as it can take you into the depths of despair over the death of a cousin or the unbridled joy of a hole-in-one on the golf course. In a linear western way, we make sense of the notion that life is full of ups and downs and that we have good times and bad times.

In a more esoteric way—understood in the patient ways of so many of the old cultures—we learn that things may not be purely branded as either up or down, or good or bad. The question we may hear if we stop to listen is;

"How do you know if something is an up or a down?"

Perhaps you failed an exam? Down. And yet, it may galvanise you to really study harder next time, or change your course to something you actually love. Up.

Maybe you buy a new car with your bonus from work? Up. However, your teenage learner driver scrapes the side on a pole during a parking exercise. Down.

In the fullness of time, and avoiding a judgement of good versus bad in the moment, the safe response by the older and wiser cultures is that things are merely a twist or a turn.

Amazingly, it is only at the turning points along the branch where new growth happens. Again, much like our lives. New shoots of possibility emerge as we are faced with challenging choices, and the berries are the fruits which appear as rewards for having navigated a time of turmoil or triumph. Crucial to the story of this branch are that two opposing thorns grow out of every node along the way. One is a shorter, hooked thorn which points backwards and reminds us to look back along our past and remember all that has brought us into this moment. The first teams and the failures, the trials and tribulations, the friends and the foes.

The second is a longer, straight thorn which points forwards and reminds us that the journey of our lives is yet to be lived; we should think about the future and where we might want to take our next step at any turning point.

The two thorns stand as perfect foils for each other. The one asks us to reflect on our past; the other one says not to become stuck there. The one says 'let's embrace the future'; the other one reminds us never to forget where we came from.

We have all had many turning points in our lives; some hugely significant, and others less meaningful. Some of them have happened through our own making, whilst others have caught us blindsided. If you're reading this, you've made it through them all so far, and you already know there will be more to come.

I remain inspired by the words of the energetic young Indian hotelier in the movie *The Best Exotic Marigold Hotel* who continues to stay calm through the chaos with the mantra:

"It will all be OK in the end. And if it's not OK, it's not the end."

Sonny Kapoor (played by Dev Patel)

There was a time in my life when things were not OK. I was halfway through my National Service and as South Africans, we were still fighting a war on two fronts. One in Angola, the other in Mozambique. Both opponents were heavily backed by the communist regimes of Russia and Cuba, and although I never fired a shot in anger, I was certainly helping to pack the cargo planes with supplies.

I am not proud of my support of an unjust system; as much as I justified my decision to blindly follow the country's laws in order to avoid a possible stint in jail, I lacked the courage to act differently. Following the crowd meant that I had perpetuated the system, and although it was a mind-blowing learning experience from which I grew enormously, my years of serving my old country could have been spent in a more dignified pursuit of the humane.

Within six weeks of my completion of a full two years of National Service, I found myself as a student at The Grand Parade in Cape Town on the 11th February 1990, celebrating the release of Nelson Mandela.

It was an epic twist and turn of global proportions.

While the camera flashes of the world's press lit up my country, I questioned why I had spent two valuable years of my life essentially supporting a system which would keep this man imprisoned. I had never seen him before, and here, in The Mother City against the backdrop of Table Mountain, he emerged as the loving Father of a nation. He became a global reference point of forgiveness and Humanity. Surrounded by thousands of dancing and jubilant fellow South Africans, and enveloped by hundreds of recently unbanned flags of the Struggle, I was at a turn in my own life in the middle of a twist for the world.

A few years later, I grabbed an opportunity to at least be in Nelson Mandela's proximity. I had no idea that I would actually meet this icon of leadership and servant of Humanity. Like many businessmen at the time, my father was invited with a colleague of his to have breakfast with President Mandela at his home in Houghton. Here was my chance, and I declared that I was going to attend too. My dad gently explained that I hadn't been invited, and so I settled for availing myself as my father's personal driver. At least I would be allowed into the gates, and I might see him standing on the steps of his home, welcoming his two visitors.

Dad deemed that as a plausible plan, and I watched from the driver's seat of his BMW as the men greeted warmly and entered the house. I am not sure exactly how many minutes later, but it wasn't more than a few pages into my book, when I noticed my father waving excitedly from the same steps and motioning for me to come quickly.

"The President wants to meet you!" he exclaimed, and as I looked up from the first step, there he was; dressed in one of his iconic shirts and smiling that enigmatic Madiba smile.

His hands seemed impossibly soft for someone who had seen so much time in a prison; who had practiced boxing as an art and a science, and had worked in a lime quarry on 'The Island'. He held both of mine in both of his as he quietly, but respectfully admonished my father, "When will your father learn that if there is a place at the breakfast table, you should not leave someone in the parking lot?"

My father and his colleague looked like scolded schoolchildren, and I felt like royalty as I was ushered to the breakfast table of four. The President pulled a chair out for me and invited me to sit, and there was no more talk of business, only a huge interest in my views as someone closer to the youth and the challenges we might be facing. It was an open door to a burning question I had sat with since the day of his release and his appearance on the Grand Parade. I took my second opportunity of the morning and asked him that question.

"Mr. President, I spent two years of my life in the South African Defence Force. Do you think my past will be held against me in the new South Africa?"

He put just the fingertips of his hands together, paused for consideration, and said something which changed my life.

"You did what you did with the information you had at the time. The real question is what are you going to do from now?"

I savoured the last of the soft eggs, seasoned with the sauce of forgiveness, and I was thankful not to have added to their saltiness from the relief of my own tears. In that moment, I saw a new path in the turning point, and my pictures of the world seemed so much clearer in the presence of new options.

"Do the best you can until you know better. Then when you know better, do better."

Maya Angelou

Six Sets of Opposing Pictures

As I have alluded to before, for half my life at the time of writing, I have lived in the Old South Africa, and for the second half, in the new one. From a system of white minority rule called Apartheid to a free and fair and fully-fledged democracy. Whilst this extraordinary country is not unique in its contrasts, it is both a shining and a stark example of so many opposing ambiguities and paradoxical polarities. We have one of the worst gaps between the wealthy and the desperate poor, and a growing trend of corruption at the highest levels. Yet, over 220 000 Non-Governmental Organisations (NGOs) registered with the Department of Social Development (Sango net pulse, April 2020). Most of them are doing the work our Government can't or won't do with extra funding by taxpayers and international donors with money they—our Government—would love to have, but hopefully will not see.

We have magnificent landscapes but high levels of environmental degradation; beautiful beaches, but lots of litter. We have stories of untold love and unspoken hatred, cringeworthy cowardice and headline heroics; we have the beautiful Big Five, battered by brutal poaching, and we have both snakes and statesmen in the seats of control. As a country, we have been shown visionary leadership from global icons and have been robbed blind by the greedy. We have shown others the light while we've been the electricians of our own darkness. This land will make you laugh from the deepest bowels of your soul, but you will also cry real tears - enough to wet your feet—even whilst wearing your veldskoene or your pategas. (Uniquely natural and very South African footwear).

There is never a dull moment and not a great deal of middle ground in South Africa and good luck trying to find a fence to sit on. The fences in this place are either the barriered dreams of demagogues and despots, barbed with brutality, or they are broken. There is little comfort here for the fence sitter. It is a country of extremes and it seems as though it has always been so. When we fly, we fly high. When we crash, we do so at speed with a rarity of safety features and even less accountability. The old adage that 'Africa is not for sissies' holds true on its Southernmost tip, which has captured more than its fair share of global interest and worldwide indignation. We have been loved and hated and loved again, but almost never ignored. We have been courted and colonised, pampered and plundered, gently tended and over tendered.

Ken Kesey, the author of the spectacular book turned movie, *One Flew Over the Cuckoo's Nest*, once remarked, "To hell with facts! We need stories."

We have stories in this country of atrocious inhumanity. We also have stories of courage, of care, and of kindness; of selfless serving, humility, humour, and hope. We have stories of Humanity. Humanity at its finest.

Without diving into an historical timeline of this sublime and ridiculous land, I have been held fascinated by these opposing attitudes and actions. The question for a long time for me has been what have been the underlying pictures which have caused these behaviours? What has been the SEE which has led to the DO?

The world I see through a microscope will be different than what I see through my own spectacles, and to that which I see through a good set of binoculars, or even a telescope. The lenses I wear will affect how I see the world, and how I see the world will influence the actions I take, and how I might behave.

For the first half of my life, I grew up in a country which favoured a particular set of lenses. To say that there wasn't another way of seeing, would be untrue; it was perhaps just a strong leaning towards more specific viewpoints which were predominant.

My favourite coastal haven, St Francis Bay in the Eastern Cape of South Africa has a prevailing westerly wind. The other winds do blow from time to time, but the predominant direction is from the West. In a similar way, the pictures I grew up with changed from time to time, but there was a primary package and a common construct which I experienced, and maybe they too, came from the West.

I am really keen to tell you the stories which I hope will illustrate these pictures and their polar opposites, so here they are. There are six of them, and each one will receive its own chapter decorated mainly by stories.

1) The world is a simple place with a single version of 'the truth'
2) The world is a finite place where only tangible things have value
3) The world is an unfriendly place
4) We are separate and disconnected from one another
5) Some of us are better than others—a world of superiority vs inferiority
6) Power (force and control) gets things done.

Being born in South Africa in the 1960s, growing up in the 70s, finishing school in the 80s and entering University and the world of work up to the mid-1990s, these were the predominant pictures which surrounded me.

And the system which used these pictures best of all, was called Apartheid.

Based on these pictures, my DO at the time was predictable. I spent two years in the South African Defence Force defending these pictures. I am not proud of that, though I learned a lot; and much of what I learned lay in a new set of lenses which I started to develop. I am learning, too, that those lenses need constant cleaning and ongoing upgrades.

Apartheid as a system ticked all these boxes. There was a simple version of the truth. There was scant value for the immeasurable quality of Humanity. 'Die Swart Gevaar' (Black Danger) and 'Reds under the beds' (Communists in your own homes) were popular phrases thrown around by political leaders to paint a dreary scenario of an unfriendly world. We were so divided as a country that people of different race groups lived in different geographical regions under the separate areas act. Superiority was based solely on skin colour, and white was right. Lastly, holding all this together was a powerful, top down command and control system which was never afraid to show its force.

Marching in the footsteps of the majority of young white men at the time, I bought in to these viewpoints. Lock, stock and barrel—and I knew how to put all three together in cleaning and reassembling a weapon.

I was an eighteen-year-old private school graduate, and I was in charge of a fully automatic assault rifle. More by luck than by design, I never had to use this weapon on any fellow human being, though I like to think I played a small role in ensuring I never did active border or township duty.

The rumour at the time during basic training, was that the best marksmen furthered their military careers by promotion to such postings. This idea was not even a blip on my own radar screen, and I was intent on laying as low as possible for the next two years. When it came to shooting practice at Rashoop—a place which the mere mention of its name still causes my hairs to stand on their anxious ends—the thought, like so many other thoughts in the army, was don't stand out of the crowd.

Never be first and never be last. Together with a few close friends—who remain some of my closest to date, and who shared this view of self-preservation—we hatched a plan;

something one learned to do quickly in the defence force.

We used some of our allotted ammunition to take pot shots at the adjacent targets on the shooting range. One direct hit out of five on one's own allocated target seemed enough to avoid a two hundred metre run with a fully loaded ammunition case, but definitely not enough to send you as a frontline marksman to defend your country.

Apart from a slightly confused nod of approval from the authorities in charge—and a broad and proud grin from the soldier who scored an astonishing six out of five—the day passed by without incident, and we could carry on in a relentless pursuit for mediocrity.

I hope the beaming private enjoyed his time on the border.

Though these were the prevailing views of the system, they were never the views of my family. On the contrary, my parents, most of my Aunts and Uncles, and certainly my cousins held different views of the world. I still look up to an older cousin I had in this world once. He died tragically in a car accident on his way back from holiday to his matric year as the head boy of Pretoria Boys High School, one of the truly great schools in South Africa. So, when I say that I look up to him, I really mean that. Many years after his death he still influences my thoughts and my actions. There were many others like him around me who saw the flipside of these six pictures, but a story lives with me still which was typical of his view of the world.

My father, Colin, and my cousin, also Colin, were avid squash players and they enjoyed a close relationship as uncle and nephew. Needless to say, the family challenge was laid down in a high stakes series which carried a deadline of young Colin's sixteenth birthday. If young Colin could beat old Colin, the family would enjoy a celebratory meal out on old Colin's account. Old Colin would have to stand up, make a toast, and admit that his nephew was a superior squash player. If young Colin failed in this quest, he would have to take out an advert in the classifieds of both the Pretoria News and Johannesburg's The Star newspapers and publicly admit his defeat to his superior uncle. For close on two years, every few months a game would be arranged and in the early battles, the squash savvy guile of experience would beat the raw energy of youth. The banter and bragging rights belonged to the old buffalo whilst the young lion would lick his wounds with a sporting smile. The family would feast together, memories were made and we looked forward greatly to the next encounter across the boerewors (farmer's sausage) curtain—the culinary and cultural line between the Southern city of Johannesburg and its Northern neighbour of Pretoria.

As the day of declaration neared, the games became closer as contests as the young lion moved the old buffalo around the court, but still there was no celebratory dinner, and a phone call to the classifieds looked inevitable for young Colin.

On the day before he turned sixteen, young Colin had a last chance to avoid public humiliation and being roasted like the rest of a substantial quantity of meat at the next family braai. (BBQ – but just way better somehow). The game wasn't even close as the young lion tore strips off the old buffalo to leave him sweating in a heap in the corner. With his heavy lungs heaving, settling for humiliation over heart attack, he was helped up by young Colin, and during a sticky embrace, Uncle Colin realised that he had been played.

He had been played by an infinite player.

Long before Simon Sinek finished school, and even before the book by James P. Carse called *Finite and Infinite Games* was published in 1986 which inspired Sinek to write *The Infinite Game*, my world had a teenage example of an infinite player.

There was little doubt that Colin junior could have beaten Colin senior in previous games, but in his eyes then, the game was over. He kept the game alive for as long as possible favouring the infinity of relationship over the finiteness of a result. Cousin Colin loved the family get-togethers, as much as anyone else, and he cherished the times, the meals and the other infinite games which would result when there were lots of friends and family gathered together before the invention of Wi-Fi or other distractive devices. Why kill the game before you can extract the full enjoyment which lives in the playing?

Just over a year later, Cousin Colin's life was over. His finite game had ended way too soon, yet in memory he lives on, lives strong, and perhaps therefor, he lives infinitely.

He shows me still that there is a flipside to all six pictures, and it is in the flipside where new possibilities reside.

1) 'The world' is a complex place and there are many versions of 'the truth'
2) 'The world' is an infinite place where intangible things carry great value
3) 'The world' is a friendly place
4) We are infinitely connected to each other
5) We are not superior or inferior, or even equal. We are all unique
6) Energy and influence inspire results.

Let's play together as we weave through these wonderings and meander with some meaning. I believe there is some truth to both sets of pictures, and that all of them lie on a continuum. As an example, let me take picture three for instance. Is the world a friendly or an unfriendly place?

The answer? You guessed it!

Yes.

If I tell my teenage daughter that we live on the extreme side of an unfriendly world, and the pictures I paint are all fear based and the SEE is untrusting, I can expect a predictable DO. No going out at night to visit friends; in fact, no going out at all. Absolutely no social get-togethers. No purchases of any sort because you can't trust anyone these days. And definitely no boyfriends. The GET is an isolated soul, a hateful hermit, and no sense of humour or Humanity.

If, on the other extreme I paint a picture of a completely friendly world, and that no harm will ever befall her, I may be irresponsible as a father. Come home when you like, wear what you want, hitch a lift with whoever you choose, somebody will always be there to tuck you in to your warm bed safely at night, and nobody would ever even think of spiking your drink. Well, the DO would be different, and the GET may be hard for any parent to contemplate.

Somewhere along that line between the two extremes, we must find a balance which works for us and our family, and it may be a different one to that found at our neighbours.

Perhaps, as we peruse through these pages, we might see that all these pictures are interlinked, and crucially, if we only see through one set of lenses, we are largely confined to one set of behaviours, and that robs us of our privilege as people in leadership and in life…

Choice.

I hope you choose to read further as we explore each of these polarities in turn knowing that there is neither a wrong nor right approach to be taken, simply a space to examine some options and ponder over a different path for a while.

As I do the same while writing, I remember an extraordinary character I played cricket against on a club tour with the Warthogs to the UK. His name was Christopher Bazalgette who bowled a humble off spin. In his own words, delivered in a glorious English accent he said:

'I simply toss it out there and it asks some questions.'

In over forty seasons with The Hampshire Hogs, and a clutch of other clubs he represented during an illustrious amateur career he has taken over 2500 wickets. Mine included.

I hope these thoughts and the stories which follow will merely ask a few questions, and that as you follow the track of your own questions you live a little closer to your own unique answer.

And if you do find yourself holing out to a fielder in the deep, or being castled by one which keeps low—just know, you are not alone.

"Live the questions now.

Perhaps you will then gradually, without noticing it,

live along some distant day into the answer.'

Rainer Maria Rilke

Let's walk out together and open the batting with a framework for these polarities of possibility.

A Framework for the Fine Line Between Polarities

Or, I guess in another way, a frame for the lenses we might be seeing through together.

Imagine a canyon with a tightrope connecting the two steep sides. The sides are the two possible extremes of any point of view. The one side might represent feelings of tension, the other side an experience closer to connection.

There is no correct place to stand at all times, and the only rule is you have to be on the rope. You cannot stand on the perceived safety of the earth, as that option doesn't exist.

You have to be somewhere on the rope between these two extremes.

As mentioned before, we will walk along six of these ropes.

TENSION (RED)	CONNECTION (BLUE)
Single truth	Multiple Truths
A Finite world	An Infinite world
An Unfriendly world	A Friendly world
We are separate and disconnected	We are infinitely connected
We are Superior or inferior	We are all unique
Power and authority get things done	Energy and influence work too

I like the use of the word polarities.

Firstly, these viewpoints are polar opposites of each other. Secondly, by definition, a polarity is not meant to be solved. Thirdly, one cannot live in isolation without the other. Like a tightrope walker, we need to find our own balance along each of these ropes all in pursuit of a loftier goal.

In this case, the higher goal might be choice.

As a facilitator of learning for more than half my life to date, I have worked with countless teams and organisations in the pursuit of many higher goals, and in keeping within the framework, I have chosen six themes which always rank as the top desired outcomes.

- Constant learning and innovation
- Generosity and sharing
- Relationship
- Integration
- Collaboration
- 'Fully charged' Engagement

My intention is that a walk between the six polarities may find you some clarity in reaching these important goals.

Please don't be hung up, no pun intended, on the colours—they are merely there to lend a simple language of lenses.

If I only look through a RED set of spectacles, I will only see a RED world.

It is when I have both the RED and the BLUE lenses, I can better exercise my options and choose a path best suited for me and others in that moment.

Another word for a tightrope walker is a funambulist.

Let's have some fun as we embrace these polarities and amble together along the fine lines between tension and connection.

And perhaps we might choose to play a little more in the BLUE and a little less in the RED?

> *"We don't see things as they are, we see them as we are."*
>
> **Anaïs Nin**

Welcome to Polarity 1. A single truth or multiple truths?

POLARITY 1

A SINGLE TRUTH OR MULTIPLE TRUTHS?

The higher goal in this first chapter is to achieve constant learning and innovation.

RED VIEW OF MORE TENSION:

'The World' is a simple place with a single version of 'the Truth'.

In this view of the world, things are either right or wrong. Black or white. You have made a profit or a loss and the answer is either Yes or No. Things are orderly, structured and largely recipe driven with strict adherence to the process and the protocol. We've all heard the line manager or school teacher who have leered through their lenses and laid out our options:

"It's my way or the Highway."

Make no mistake, I have been that father too at times, and as these pictures unfold, and as I've alluded to before, I hope to share that none of them are wrong per se, their effectiveness may simply be dependent on the situation at hand. There are times when there is a correct and single answer, and it is important to possess great clarity in the moment. In the world of animal tracking, one needs to know the difference between a white rhino spoor and a black rhino spoor. There is not a multiple version of this truth in this instance, and knowing the single right answer might keep you well away from harms door.

BLUE VIEW TOWARDS CONNECTION:

'The World' is a complex place with multiple versions of 'the Truth'.

Through this lens we can accept the ambiguity which lies at the heart of different viewpoints.

If this is my 'SEE', then my 'DO' is to listen with curiosity,

And the 'GET' is an increase in learning and potential innovation.

To illustrate the shift along this continuum, I'd like to tell you some stories where you will enjoy a meal with my Godfather who reminds me that there is more than one truth to the way we learn. We will travel to Central Park, New York where we might learn that sticking doggedly to a single version of the truth may end up in phoning 911 to arrest a peaceful birdwatcher. We will go tracking together and observe that while the real tracks of the animals left in the sand never lie, our interpretations may vary greatly. Next up will be a story of how just a small shift in the dial on our radio station can lead to far greater clarity. Let's ride with Mpumi, a young man who has pivoted his bicycle tour business into a last mile delivery service, and in the process helped me to see new possibility in my own business. We will see a different truth in a tattoo, and that there is more than one way to get into your car; we will round off this chapter with a poem from Humphrey who reminds us that we need both knowledge and character as multiple truths, and lastly, let's learn a lesson from the martial art of stick fighting.

Stay curious and take your time. If you rush too quickly, you may close off the possibility of a different truth, and that is what this chapter is all about.

"Everyone in a complex system has a slightly different interpretation. The more interpretations we gather, the easier it becomes to gain a sense of the whole."

Margaret Wheatley

Enjoy!

Guiding Principles

I have been blessed with many special relationships in my life and I enjoyed a memorable dinner with one of them some years ago in Cape

Town's Local Grill restaurant in Salt River. Like all great meals, there is always something more to it than just the food or service. The company you enjoy and the conversations which flow are the real Hallmarks of a great meal out.

Uncle Butch is not my uncle at all, but he is my Godfather, and I've always learned heaps from him even though for most of our lives we have lived in different cities. He provided me with a lifelong lesson when he said that there were really only two ways to learn things properly. The first was through the hard knocks of life. The second was at the feet of the master.

He would then gently remind me that the first was often infinitely more painful than the second. Ever since then I've kept my ears well open when in conversation with Uncle Butch, and Monday night in a Cape Town winter was no exception.

The 2014 Brazilian World Cup had ended the night before, and the cool, clinical Germans had swept up all before them, including the coveted trophy in a deserved procession of footballing professionalism. The talk inevitably turned to sports, and Uncle Butch started to comment about some of his observations both as a spectator and as a player in the aquatic version of the game known as water polo. As a marine biologist he always was more comfortable in water.

Uncle Butch always listens more than he talks, and so when he does talk, I listen. And this is what I learned.

There are, he thought, three main guiding principles to these sports. There are many, many rules which should be obeyed of course, but only three main principles which should be practiced to triumph. Not wanting to interrupt the first lesson, I tucked into my medium rare T bone with about the same relish as Luis Suarez had dined on his underdone Italian counterpart.

Firstly, you never pass the ball to someone in a worse position than you.

This was met with much head nodding, and some discussion about what this might mean as a metaphor for everyday life. How often do we see our politicians throw the proverbial hospital pass down their hallways and hierarchies? Corporate execs flee from their ivory towers in helicopters with their bonuses in tact but the business in tatters. Sportsmen and women are thrown to the lions without even a modicum of support from their administrators.

Blame blossoms and accountability evaporates as everyone from Marikana to the media looks for and attempts to shoot the few remaining scapegoats in a field of sheep. The old adage of "Not my problem" has become a well sung line out of the International Anthem, as the dreary armies of the disengaged squeeze their sponges and journey on in the pursuit to do less with more.

It was time to order a glass of the Cape's finest to wash down a well-aged product from what is deservedly rated as South Africa's best steakhouse. I was also about to digest the second lesson.

Always find a space and play into that space.

The concept of space seemed most ironic at this particular point. After 600 grams of a Tim Noakes bucket list item, accompanied by the obligatory Local Grill extras, I had none. Too full to talk, I merely listened.

The great successes of life and sports seem to be in people finding space. Or in businesses, communities or even families finding space for that matter. We spoke of niches, of people who chartered new waters, or of cricketers finding new ways to play challenging deliveries. Innovation is all about finding a space and playing into that space. Why, after all is it wise to enter an already saturated market with the same old products? David slew Goliath when he claimed his space as a slinger in artillery, not as a swordsman in heavy infantry. Solid relationships seem to find, as Kahlil Gibran so beautifully puts it, 'spaces in their togetherness'.

Great centres in rugby seem to not only find space, but create it. Even when marked by many, the great footballers conjure up a way to shake the defence and the off sides trap. Some people we spoke of had recently blossomed as they had found their space in the world, and seemed to set free their shackles as they played, and I mean played not just worked into that space. We wondered if some of our schools created space for uniqueness, or if there was space round the dinner table for differing opinions. It was Einstein who observed that space and time were essentially the same thing, so maybe, if we want more time, we need to create more space. I wondered what and who were occupying my space? They didn't always seem to be the same things which took up my time.

There is always space for a cleansing Irish coffee with Tim's full cream, and I sipped slowly on the delicacy whilst savouring it along with the third lesson.

If you don't take shots you'll never win.

Have a go sometimes; even if you have to take a risk along the way. The successful teams in the World Cup may have had a solid defence, but I'm willing to bet my next steak that the real winners also took many shots on goal.

Nick Faldo once won an Open Championship with a full house of eighteen pars in the final round. Solid, dependable, nothing flashy; but even he would have known when to take certain shots on, and when to risk.

This doesn't mean recklessness, but rather a measured confidence born from both practice and belief. I wondered how often I had left putts short on the greens of my own life. Times when I didn't put up my hand for fear of vulnerability, where the certain side-lines of comfort seemed so much more pleasurable than the playground of possibility.

The fear of writing the book seems so overwhelming that we stop even writing an essay. Or a letter. We might argue that if we do nothing, we do nothing wrong, and therefore when our will comes into existence, we leave this place a little safer. Surely though we also leave it a little poorer without our contribution.

Taking a shot at our own goals is imperative if we are ever to hit them, and that means to dare to fail sometimes. So, ask that someone special to dance; build your own bucket list, pull out the driver on a reachable par four once in a while, sing with your kids in the car. Travel without an itinerary, or have the odd meeting with no agenda.

It's never comfortable to say I tried and I failed, but I'm sure it's worse to say "I wish I had."

There is often magic in the unknown, and when it finds some space to shine, it can light up the world. Just ask a humble herd boy who years later took a shot at wearing a number 6 rugby jersey, and amongst other things changed the world.

Fine wine and a well-aged steak are luxuries, but when they are washed down with wisdom, they become a privilege.

The rules may be there for a reason, but guiding principles are there for a purpose.

I look forward to my next lesson from the feet of the master.

A Better Set of Lenses

Let me tell you a story about Christian Cooper and Amy Cooper.

They are not "The Coopers" family. They are unrelated in a host of different ways, but they share a surname and a recent incident in Central Park in New York City.

Christian is out birdwatching. He has a bicycle helmet attached to his belt and he looks like he regularly works out. He has a neat pair of steel rimmed spectacles and he peers into the foliage of the protected area of this iconic park known as The Ramble. Christian is searching for a checklist of the 230 species of birds found in this haven amidst the hustle. The Ramble is thirty-eight acres of a 'wild garden' and was set aside as early as 1857 in the Greensward plan as a refuge away from carriage drivers. (Wikipedia)

For over one hundred-and-sixty years people have wandered and wondered through this natural area without any irritation from traffic—cyclists included, which is a real blessing in a bustling city. It is a peaceful place and it openly and freely invites peaceful people. Apart from the other rules and regulations which govern this cosmopolitan playground, The Ramble only has one other request. Dogs to be leashed at all times in The Ramble. Fair enough I would think, it is after all a nature reserve.

Enter Amy Cooper. With her dog. And no leash.

Christian lowers his Swarovski binoculars, the brand being an important part of my reflection in this case, and politely asks Amy to put her dog on leash. She says the other runs are closed and the dog needs his exercise. He suggests some other areas. She says they are too dangerous. He repeats the law and points her to the obvious signage around the park. Her mood becomes slightly more heated, he starts to video her reaction, and she loses the plot completely.

In a dramatic ninety second display of desperation, Amy is on the line to 911. Her life and the life of the dog is being threatened by a man in Central Park. Christian stands his ground and continues to video with the steady hand of a birdwatcher. Amy's dog tries to stand his ground too, but most of his legs are airborne as she holds him by his collar in her theatrics which are worthy of a show on nearby Broadway. It is only the actions of the owner which are threatening the life of the dog in a brutal choke hold, one which would become famously banned due to the ramifications of an incident on the same day in Minnesota. 25th May 2020, George Floyd.

The case of the Central Park "Karen", a wonderful acronym which I will write up as a P.S., was 'unleashed' and nurtured by social media where it will fuel the fires and fan the flames of demanding debate for years to come. Amy Cooper's amateur audition and moment of madness designed as a drama, ends as comedic in the viewing. It is almost laughable.

Except that it isn't.

Christian is black. Amy is White.

Maybe all the superiority she exhibited in that random meeting in The Ramble is depicted in that short sentence.

lowercase black. Uppercase White.

I wonder if she had just stopped long enough to greet this man whether she might still have her job. I wonder if she had just apologised and put the lead on her dog whether she wouldn't have a case against her for issuing a false report. I wonder if she had just noticed for a second, his magnificent set of Swarovski binoculars, whether she might have taken a look through a truly superior set of lenses. But perhaps that is a step too far for a non-birder?

If I am to change my behaviour, I have to look through different lenses. I need to see that the world is not always unfriendly when someone of colour approaches me for anything, let alone to obey the law. I need to see that there is more than one way of seeing, and that there is no way to solve the polarity between equality and superiority other than by embracing the higher order of uniqueness. I need to know that we are infinitely connected, and that defaulting to calling the police or just writing more policy will only keep us more separate and disconnected.

Change needs new pictures. If I only see one road, I only have one destination, and with only one map, I am robbed of that which makes me human: choice.

How do I choose a different response if I consult a single script?

If we could look through the unique lenses we each carry, we might be swept up in the excitement of the sighting of a Red-tailed Hawk in The Ramble.

We might see a far clearer picture, not because of the Swarovski lenses, but through the aperture of Humanity. I will see my own inner 'Karen', not through more expensive equipment and increasing legislation, but through the eyes of others, and being able to choose the better set of lenses.

I hope that I meet Christian Cooper, and that when I do, we will not be black or white.

We will simply be Birdwatchers.

With lots to teach and maybe a whole host more to learn? And isn't that exciting? For what we teach, we probably know already, but what we learn is up to that moment, as yet undiscovered.

Christian, please come birdwatching in South Africa…

… and don't forget to bring your binoculars!

P.S. An Acronym for KAREN

K Know your rights

A Accuse everyone

R Request a manager

E Escalate to Authority

N Neglect reason

With these as your only set of pictures, it may explain why we end up losing our job, our dog, and our minds?

I wonder if we could be a different "KAREN".

K Know your neighbour

A Appreciate everyone

R Respect opinion

E Embrace uniqueness

N Never stop learning

It might result in a better world?

Lessons in the Sand

Everything leaves a track. It is the mark of our presence, an acknowledgement of our impact on this earth. We can map out where we have been, what we have consumed and where we have shopped. We can work out with whom we have been and with whom we haven't. and as we look back over the twists and turns of the many branches of our journeys, we can see clearly the mistakes we have made or the opportunities we have grasped. The stories of our lives can be pieced together like intricate tapestries which would make for some interesting reading in reflection as we follow the pathways of our own puzzles.

Yes, everything leaves a track, and all of us are trackers. We are all trying to follow something. We are looking for signs and signals to show us the way. Our curiosity is fuelled by connections and clues, and we search for the roads to reward or redemption. Or maybe even revenge. Financial aficionados are constantly challenged by the numbers which should be in the balance sheet, but may be struck dumb by those that are not.

Marketers scratch beneath the surface to understand where consumers are moving and migrating towards, and Doctors follow the symptoms of sickness to prescribe the correct cure. Weathermen and women send up their balloons, Rock Drill Operators follow reefs rich in ore, and Air Traffic Controllers scrutinise their screens as if other's lives depended on them. For they do. Every minute of every day.

Tracking has been described as the oldest science known to man. It is a science because it relies on memory and it insists on rigorous procedure. There is a logical and rational process to be followed in a pursuit of patterns and probability. Things can be measured, and if we are not sure of the answer, we can embark on a systematic sequence of signs and a dogged deciphering of dents to determine what walked here. Or ran. Or slithered. Or hopped. Or jumped. Or maybe disappeared completely as even animals which fly leave a track sometimes. People that have never walked in the African bush before have identified the spoor of zebra because they have ridden horses. Warthogs, because they have farmed with pigs, and buffalo because of walking in fields of cattle. The structure of a cat's paw doesn't surprise many, but out here, it is the size of that paw which takes one's breath away.

But tracking is also an art. And art encourages imagination and a sense of what might be? It is as much a challenging of the question than it is of hunting the answer. Art is core intuition or gut feel. Art is interpretive and it thrives in an inkling. It is make-believe which entices us to make and dares us to believe. A whimsical brush stroke of an almost imperceptible shift in the breeze causes a change to the canvas of clairvoyance as the story transforms to an entirely new possibility. A hundred pages might be worth less than a hunch, and an instinct may give birth to an idea.

It has been said that the !Kung people from the Kalahari Desert were some of the best trackers on the planet. Tracks and signs in the schoolroom of the sand would be remembered long into their adult life, and their powers of observation would be play acted through a theatrical pursuit of their prey. Upright postures with extended necks would be adopted for taller animals, whilst their gait would change for those with noses close to the ground. The tracker who most understood the animal may well have specialised in the following of that animal. It seemed it was much easier to find them if one was already in their skin.

Perhaps they practiced empathic tracking?

Seeing with the eyes of the other.

Hearing with the ears of the other.

Feeling with the heart of the other.

We speak often of the crucial ingredient of connection in leadership. These people have taken it a sandy step further for centuries.

They know that connection is essential for life.

Every time I go tracking, I learn more; primarily about myself. This time, it was a stark and humbling lesson. I was with Darryl Dell, one of the finest guides in the world and we were taking a tracking group for a walk on a Tuesday morning.

Since my first tracking experience I have loved this challenge of the meeting of the left and right hemispheres of logic and imagination—this blend between science and art, which is tracking. The small tracks hold as much allure as the big ones, and when we encountered a perfect set of chameleon tracks beautifully embedded in the early morning sand, I was thrilled. Thrilled because I knew this track, and also because they were so distinct, maybe we'd find the actual creature and remove all doubt.

When Darryl said he could see the animal, I intensified my gaze into the branches and stems of the young silver cluster leaf. Flapped necked chameleons can be pretty small and highly camouflaged, so I inspected every folded leaf from every angle and most importantly in this case, a dangerous amount of confidence.

By this stage Darryl was looking at me rather quizzically, and had asked whether I had seen it yet?

Doubt had not yet entered my mind, and as a consequence, my doggedness grew into a determination to achieve the right result. Even when Renata—a delegate who had taken to tracking like a frightened and sunburned hippo takes to water—shrieked with delight and pointed to the base of the bush, my first thought was, "No ways, it can't be."

Well, it was. There, right up against the main small trunk, and still half covered by grass in the sand was the tiniest of leopard tortoises—no bigger than an original Lions match box!

In those few seconds, I learned enough to fill a field guide. Maybe even a field guide to life?

- If you follow the tracks of the animal, you will find the animal who left the tracks.

There is no getting around this. No matter how much you want to find a chameleon, if you're tracking a tortoise, you will find a tortoise. Please apply your own lessons here; you may find there are many.

- Be clear about what you are tracking, otherwise you end up looking in the wrong places.

Tortoises do not climb trees. Not even small shrubs. Period.

- Over confidence and sticking stubbornly to a set of beliefs may take you down an unwanted and irreversible path.

This is a bit like getting on a train bound for Cape Town and hoping you will arrive in Durban. The tracks are laid out and the journey in this case has a predetermined destination.

- The newest recruit may have the best answer.

Whilst experience can be invaluable, so too can fresh eyes. They are unencumbered by the wrong experience. Sometimes thirty years of experience is not always a good thing—especially if I have been walking unaware and practicing bad habits. I have had over forty years of playing golf. For a glorious month in my enjoyment of this journey I was a four handicap—I am now a twelve. Go figure!!

- If my ego is attached to my outcomes, I may be in trouble.

Pretending to have seen the tortoise and then covering up my search in the branches as a quest to find a chameleon as well, would be nothing short of lying to protect my image.

Inauthenticity is not a desired trait in any leadership book, blog or banter.

- Jumping to conclusions may lead me to a dead-end.

A conclusion is exactly that. An end. When I jump to a conclusion, there is no more room for open debate, learning, or exploration. The matter or lesson is concluded. Put to rest. Signed and sealed. Right or wrong. Black or white. Tick or cross.

But that doesn't happen with learning or with life. Learning doesn't end when the school bell rings for the lesson to be over, and I've always been intrigued, when hearing at the end of a reading from the Bible in church at the announcement,

"Here endeth the lesson."

Surely the learning should continue?

I wonder why no one in the thousands of years of the Bible, with its multiple authors, psalms, parables, letters, verses, chapters and books hasn't stopped to change track and look at the difference between a finite and an infinite world?

Whilst a finite world may be measured by the number of lessons read or delivered, an infinite world would track the impact of the learning.

And that may be never-ending.

- We learn as much from our failures as we do from our successes. But only if we admit to them and own them.

I doubt whether I will make the same mistake again—not when it comes to a small tortoise track. Like a battle wound, the scar tissue of every short-gaited scratch is etched in every minute detail into the data warehouse of my left brain.

- Lifelong learning happens when there is space given for it to unfold.

Darryl could have told us what the track was before we'd even seen it. He could have pointed out the tiny tortoise and moved on in an effort to accumulate more ticked tracks. Pointing to each at a professional pace he might have reeled them off: Leopard, male, tick. White rhino, white not black, tick. Jackal, tick. Frog, tick. Thank you, see you at breakfast, tick.

Instead, he gave us space to explore the avenues of our own awareness and annals of our own archives. You don't reach this level of learning through the mere dishing out of constant lessons.

My learning from that seemingly insignificant moment with that still impossibly small tree climbing tortoise with chameleon shoes continues onwards, and if you've followed this far, so too will yours.

Learning is indeed a lifelong journey, and the tracking of that journey is best taken with the whole brain, and as the artistic scientists of the !Kung people might remind us…

It is helped by an open heart.

Just Touch the Dial

The oven of life heats up gradually. Tempers are tested with each travesty in the traffic and the city spits out its acerbic toxicity. Perhaps it is just coincidental that 'toxic' and 'city' find a cynical mix in toxicity, but in the February heat of Johannesburg, the pace sometimes feels rather poisonous. The political promises are padding up to pre-election propaganda, and each passing newspaper billboard uncovers another story of mismanagement and corruption.

To add more darkness to these matters, we also have load shedding.

Already stretched businesses and families are asked to pay more taxes with less electricity. To feed more mouths with less fuel and to do more homework by fading torch light. What little light we may be seeing at the end of the tunnel is shut off for another tranche of time as we worry about frozen goods perishing. The buzzing inside our own heads is dulled and sometimes deafened by the incessant drone of the diesel generators which jump to life in the neighbourhoods of the well prepared. We are not one of those households as yet, but at least one upside is that this lack of power supply also pushes the automatic pause button on the CNN news feeds which seem only to add to the venom of a volatile world. We are temporarily blissfully unaware of the surrounding uncertainty, we care less about complexity, and as for ambiguity, well, it seems arbitrary with a lack of options.

Being in the sparkless darkness of my own downward-spiralling demeanour, I had not yet begun to appreciate the simplicity of life with a Consol glass solar lamp, a warm family conversation and no arguments over the shutting down of two teenagers' devices in time for bed. In our near addiction for digital connection, perhaps we were losing our human one?

My temperament metre was still flickering dangerously close to tantrum level. It was another late school lift made later by the manual opening of garage doors and driveway gates, and even the car radio was crackling with distortion. This bloody load shedding has clearly even affected the broadcast of a half decent radio station in Hot 91.9 FM, and now I was going to miss the 'Old School News' by Simon Hill.

"FFS this place is a joke!"

"Just touch the dial, Dad."

With nothing to read on her own device, my fourteen-year-old daughter had noticed that the station reading was on 91.85. Not 91.9.

All it took was one touch. It did not need to be reprogrammed or twisted through a number of turns. I didn't need to buy a new radio and it had nothing to do with load shedding.

I was back in the 'Cool of Old School' and we could giggle through another superb creation of the Old School News.

The drive to school was a joy, and we were not late. Someone even let me in to the busy lane of Oxford road with a smile and a wave, and I had time to enjoy a good coffee as the needle of own internal boiling levelled off to moderate and for a rare moment may even have touched on being calm.

I sit here and wonder with the same coffee, whether I just need to touch the dial of my own life sometimes? I don't need a big fix, and my career doesn't need a drastic change. I don't need a total overhaul of my physical or mental states. Just a small nudge or a slight reminder.

We are tempted so often to work on the 91.85. To rebrand the business, to re-engineer the culture. Recapitalise the balance sheets, rebuild the Head Office and refurbish the work spaces. Most of those things are already there, and because they carry great strategic weight, the subtleties of fine tuning are mostly written off as soft skills and assigned to a largely toothless department which shouldn't need teeth in the first place.

Yet fine tuning comes for free. It comes with a smile during a greeting. It is there in the half a minute of focused attention we give to the response to our own questions. It is present in the mindful breath we take, or the stretched limbs during a tea break. When we stop long enough to capture the rays of a setting sun, or help someone with their overhead compartment luggage, we make space for the moments which truly matter, and when we say Thank You from a full heart, we lubricate the flow of social cohesion. When we sit together during a funeral in pools of pure emotion, and we say nothing individual, but feel everything together, we are fine tuning relationships which have been built over years, and we are rebuilding them with the strength of our collective silence.

Pema Chödrön is an American Tibetan Buddhist. In a YouTube clip called '*Lousy World*' she paints a beautiful analogy from the teachings of the Indian Buddhist monk Shantideva who talks of the discontent we all feel with the world at times. We walk through this harsh landscape with its discomfort and hurt our feet with its thorns, cut glass and hot sand. We are tempted to cover the whole path in leather so as to remove all irritations and walk pain free. We would not be upset by pesky ticks or corrupt politicians. We could remove all the things that bothered us and live a happy, content life.

Great idea, though impractical. The question of wisdom comes with asking why we don't just wrap that leather around our own feet. In so doing we carry our protection from within instead of trying to change the outside world. We can lean with some comfort into the discomfort, some certainty into the uncertainty, and we regulate our own temperature level through touching our own dial.

91.85 is covering the world with leather whilst 0.05 is making your own shoes, and that is so much more energy intelligent.

Just touching the dial for that extra 0.05 could make all the difference between clutter and clarity. Between distortion and direction.

It certainly turned my cynical smirk into a smile, and I let the next person through into the same busy lane of traffic.

Riding the Cycle

Perhaps it has taken a small cruel virus to open my eyes. This invisible thing has brought a new clarity to the vision I once had but maybe didn't notice enough. Covid-19 arrived unwanted and indiscriminate, and no amount of border protection or customs officials could stem the tragedy of its travels. Through no fault of their own, some businesses have been wiped out. Through no brilliance of their own, others have flourished. And somewhere in between, an army of resilient people have continued to save young children from the streets or tilled the soils of their inner-city farms. Somewhere between the heads and tails of the coin toss of Covid's fate, artists continue to conjure up a culinary magic from the kitchens of this city's streets, and brave people take one vulnerable step after the next as they find a precarious balance on the tightrope of their own lives.

They savour each sip of the air above the abyss, not daring to look down and they pray for the rope to hold each day.

We met all these people in an emotional day. And we met them all on line.

My work before Covid offered me the extraordinary privilege of spending live time with many of these leaders, and since then I have found it challenging to really enjoy what I do. I have missed the connections, the stories and the warm heart of Africa and its hugs. I have longed for the looks on our delegates' faces as they become wrapped up in the lives of these everyday heroes and heroines.

My salary was supplemented by huge job satisfaction when the embracing of emotions resulted in empathy, and when people looked through fresh eyes—primarily at themselves—there was a dividend of understanding and a thirteenth cheque of a new possibility.

All that went away with this miserable global invader. Including the salary, and any hope of a dividend. There never has been the luxury of a thirteenth cheque in my own business. I felt like I was one of those souls shuffling along the shaky string of survival.

Until I connected with these extraordinary ordinary people again. On line.

In a pioneering collaboration with a leading business school and an International Bank, our team at Lead with Humanity put together a virtual immersion. That sounds like a fun run, a silent scream or controlled chaos. An oxymoron. Seriously funny.

And yet it worked. Perfectly imperfect, as any immersion should be.

We met Mam' Khanyi at the Home of Hope who is still saving street children through this pandemic. We went farming with Ma Refiloe in her inner-city farm as she feeds her community not only with health, but also with hope. We visited Sanza in his Yeoville kitchen who not only cooked for us, but kept us enthralled with his energy and spellbound by his storytelling.

As we met all these people, I could feel my old life returning, my heart full of purpose and my lungs full of the air above the abyss. I felt more surefooted in the unsteady uncertainty of the wobbly wire of Wi-Fi. I was walking the tightrope and for the first time in months, I experienced the "fun" in being a funambulist. A tightrope walker. Each of these spectacular superheroes who have no need for capes, should be the subject of books on leadership, not just off the cuff mentions in an online immersion.

We would meet someone else today who was riding this cycle. Mpumelelo (Mpumi) Mtinsto is the entrepreneur behind *book Ibhoni*, a bicycle tour operator in Soweto. He proudly tells as that "Ibhoni" is township slang for a bicycle, and like so many in the tourism industry he was on the wrong side of this global coin toss. Facing a booking sheet which was being erased before his eyes, he found the one green chamber in a roulette wheel of Black and Red. He would pivot his tour company into a last mile delivery service. And he would use his bicycles to do this. He and his peloton of peddlers would go where the courier companies couldn't or wouldn't. His success lies in knowing his terrain. He knows every unnumbered house, every back road through the roadworks, and every possible gangster.

He is completely connected. And he and his team delivered eighteen lunches across the city of Johannesburg from the mercurial and magical Sanza, all on beautiful ceramic platters with an array of homemade drinks and a generous helping of herbs from the garden of Ma Refiloe picked with passion.

He is riding the cycle. And seemingly, he is loving the ride.

We signed off knowing that we had taken a step into our own future, and that emotions are still real even on a virtual platform. But overwhelmingly, the group still longed to physically hug Mam' Khanyi, kick the soil and get good earth under the finger nails with Ma Refiloe and sit with Sanza and share from the abundance of his platter and his person.

And of course, to be led through the streets of Soweto by Mpumi, when we conquer this coward called Covid.

Drained, but with a feeling of being alive I hadn't experienced for months, I walked into my daughter's room, and typically it was full of music. A song was playing which only served to confirm that sometimes there is a perfect order to the synchronicity of things. It was from the soundtrack to *The Greatest Showman;* originally written I think by Michelle Williams.

Tightrope.

"Some people long for a life which is simple and planned.

Tied with a ribbon.

Some people won't sail the sea 'cos they're safer on land.

To follow what's written.

But I'd follow you to the great unknown

Off to a world we could call our own.

…We're walking a tightrope."

So, if you feel that you're walking a tightrope, keep walking.

And Mpumi, as you ride this cycle, keep pedalling.

P.S. According to Wikipedia, the "fun" in funambulist is not the kind of fun associated with enjoyment, but rather from Latin origin 'funis' which means rope. Ambulate is to walk. A rope walker.

If we are to walk these ropes though, I guess it wouldn't harm to have fun in the process?

Forwards lived be must it
But backwards understood
Be only can Life

Kierkegaard Soren

Havelock is an informal settlement nestled in amongst the middle-class suburbia of Durban North. It is named after the road it has emerged from, and yet strangely the closer road is Sanderson. Sanderson is where the bread truck comes to deliver beer. Where the illegal electrical wires cross overhead to feed vital information to the community of two hundred and four structures and give life to many more cell phones. It is a dead-end road where for many, life begins, and where children play amongst the masses of meddling mechanics.

It is a place of hopeless hope with seemingly no future yet it has been there for a number of decades. People here have apparently nothing and yet have most of what they need and it is a 'slum' where the inhabitants smile through their lack of possessions. A sense of humour in a ditch of despair.

If a paradox is where two equal but opposite truths can live comfortably side by side, then Havelock is surely a paradox. Dangerous yet safe. Poor in assets yet rich in relationships. Illegal electricity yet a moral energy. Dirty river yet spotlessly clean clothes. Havelock on Sanderson.

Beer from a bread truck.

There is enough space for the temple like truck to turn in amongst a scrapyard of old parked cars, the owners of which are considered the lucky few. Occupying the shadiest morning spot adjacent to the ablution structures stands an Opel Ascona. By the looks of it in its current state, it may have been the first one ever to roll off the production line. It seems unable to roll anywhere now.

The main body is of a faint mustard hue, but could have been any colour at birth, and most of the pale-yellow paint has been stained by a bath ring of rust. The rear wiper blade has clearly wiped its last and is equally rusted fast in a final defiant middle-finger-like salute and the sound installation sticker has outlasted any semblance of sound equipment inside—but only just. Like the front number plate, it too is peeling like the yellowed wrapping of an old Ram golf ball, and there is not a single corner of lights left unbroken.

Precious little is left of the upholstery, and it seems to be disappearing faster than The Great Barrier Reef. It consists of the same bleached foam follicles that were once contained by synthetic seat covers—the easy wipe, finely punctured plastic which makes naked thighs sweat.

The sun damaged dashboard is as rough as the tyres are smooth; there is no discernible mirror on the left-hand side, and the exhaust hangs about as close to the ground as the mischievously planted tin cans on a newly-wed couple's getaway car. We would discover that the entire exhaust structure was purely ornamental as a feature.

And yet, with all the unroadworthy death trappings so clearly evident to even an untrained eye, there hangs from the driver's seat, neatly draped and perfectly pressed in its irony, a safety vest. Not an internal air bag in sight, yet the obvious presence of a safety vest, resplendent in its iridescent lime green netting with orange trimming. This would lead one to a conclusion that there is less danger being inside this vehicle than the many times spent by the driver standing on the road between breakdowns. We gave the scene a wider berth.

Perhaps a safety vest is the most obvious piece of equipment to own in a vehicle which must spend an inordinate amount of time resting between intended destinations?

There were many lessons to be enjoyed in the car itself, but the learning really ramped up at the arrival of its owner. It was a Sunday morning, but I think he was still into Saturday night. Half-awake and half-dressed he shuffled in a surprisingly energy efficient manner and like a professional fencer standing 'En Garde' he scored a perfect hit with his first advance-lunge as the key slid perfectly into the slot of its target between two bullet hole sized ruptures of rust. There was a great deal of jiggling as if he was committing hara-kiri on his own car until the bowels of the vehicle opened. He had accessed the trunk and began to lift the hatchback high into the brightening sky whilst keeping his gaze firmly in the dark holes where the speakers once resided. It is a universal truth that darkness is golden for aching retinas. Much like the speakers, the hydraulics of the hatchback had long since gone to spare parts Heaven, and a carved stick, doubling no doubt as a knobkerrie, was hastily inserted as a strut to keep the back door open.

If the first foray was about fencing, the next stage of the unfolding operation was all about gymnastics with some yoga thrown in for good measure. Entering through the back was much like a slow-motion tumble turn, and he displayed both dexterity and precision as he avoided the supporting stick. An errant move here might have had the rusted hatchback come down like a guillotine and sever off his protruding legs from the back of the knees down. The gymnast morphed into a downward dog position as his torso bent over the back seat, and then twisted into a warrior pose as the high hand looped over and unlocked the left back door.

The entire process was reversed on exiting, and it looked like the wriggling of a rabbit from the jaws of a python—again with great care not to kick the stick. The trunk was slammed shut by gravity alone once the strut was removed, and the new entrance became the recently unlocked rear left door.

From there, things turned a touch more athletic as a classic hurdle style was employed to clear the front seats. In the spirit if not the elegance of Ed Moses, who incidentally never lost a 400m hurdle race for nine years, nine months and nine days, he managed this, though was in no danger of beating neither the hurdling great's symmetry nor his record.

The right front driver's door was duly unlocked from the inside, but amazingly could now only be opened from the outside, and so the hurdle was reversed—now that might have impressed Ed Moses himself!

Who needs an alarm and anti-hijacking system when only the mystical Harry Houdini could have emulated such a body twisting and mind-bending manoeuvre?

At last! In the correct seat with the key in the ignition, it would take over twenty turns of a rapidly depleting battery and a helping hand from his mates to start the car. In a cloud of smoke and with the roar of an exhausted exhaust, he hit reverse, narrowly missing the bread truck, and came to a grinding halt some eighty metres up Sanderson Road where his helping hands gathered to inspect the hood.

On our leadership experiences we talk not about one journey, but perhaps as many as five which our delegates might venture along during our time together.

There is the journey **backwards**—where reflection over lessons learned from our past are paramount. Which relationships have truly mattered, and what moments have been sacred as memories?

Of course, this means there is a journey **forwards** along the straight spike of the Zizyphus Mucronata, the Buffalo Thorn which guides our way into the future through the setting of goals and the living of values.

The journey **inwards** is a search for the real and the Genuine Me. The shadow of our Seriti* which is significant through its dignified potential and the shadow which never leaves me.

Paradoxically, the journey **outwards** is equally important as it inspires us to venture into a quantum world, to be vulnerable and to stretch ourselves out of our comfort zones and to begin to touch the possibilities we yearn for.

And lastly, this is not a selfish journey, as it is taken with others in the journey **together**. No man is an island, and the spirit of Ubuntu* is always at play whether we notice it or not. A person is indeed only a person in the context of other people.

In perhaps five minutes of fascination, we had watched someone go on all of these journeys. It was not always easy to decipher whether forwards were backwards, or inwards was outwards, but it was a dynamic lesson so apt in the context of a paradoxical place. It ended with a mechanical conversation with others, and yet it carries on still in our memories.

Something ends, yet it lives on.

The king is dead. Long live the king.

There was another lesson here, and that was that there may be more than one way to do something. Leadership too comes in multiple shapes and forms.

There is more than one version of the truth—even to the act of getting into and starting an old Opel Ascona 1.8GLs.

I wonder if I don't sometimes give up too easily when the obvious way seems blocked. When the conventional method doesn't work. Could I use paper when a PowerPoint presentation to an executive audience fails due to a lack of electricity, and can I try a softer tone with my children when the shouting falls on deaf ears—maybe because of the shouting they have been subjected to.

Why should I not buy a safety vest—even in the hope that I never have to use it?

Perhaps I will only understand some of these things in a retrospective look along the hooked thorn of the journey backwards, but I will only able to live this life forwards.

From this moment on...

...even if it is in reverse!

As he walked through the forests of Denmark, Kierkegaard knew this from a long time ago and we are still learning. But I do know one proud man who has lost a brother and now has this quote tattooed along the front of his left shoulder.

He will never forget his treasured relationship through the reflection of deep understanding but he cannot be stuck on that journey.

He will continue to take brave steps every day and live his life forwards.

As must we all.

"Livet forstås baglœns, men må leves forlœns." The mark on Mark.

(Life can only be understood backwards, but it must be lived forwards.) Soren Kierkegaard

*Seriti is an isiSotho word describing the shadow of significance we cast as human beings. In a sense, it is the metaphysical aura we carry with us, and is seen as a result of dignity and viewed with respect.

Three interesting aspects to the concept are that firstly, only the things which are real cast the shadow. No material assets or possessions add any value to the shadows we cast. Secondly, no one's shadow is more important than another. Where our shadows overlap it simply means we have shared a part of the journey together, and that is holy ground between us. Lastly, the shadow remains long after the person passes away. We remember people through their shadows of significance, and the impact they have had on the rest of our mortal lives. The shadow, or Seriti, is the legacy we leave. In isiZulu, the concept is referred to as 'isiThunzi'.

*Ubuntu is a concept of connection and togetherness.

The full phrase is 'Umuntu Ngumuntu Ngabantu'—A person is only a person in the context of other people.

Knowledge without Character

The trolley of refreshments would be waiting just outside the classrooms of the Global Leadership Centre. Neatly stacked on its two stories would be jugs of fresh water, bowls of mints, and on Fridays a few chocolate treats to indulge the taste buds of the delegates. Behind that trolley, if we were lucky, would be the smiling Humphrey, eager to come in during a break and refresh the room.

He worked slickly with an efficiency which was admirable, and once done, he would only leave the room as soon as the delegates draped in for the next session. I asked him once why he didn't leave the room with the same efficiency with which he had refreshed it. His reply spoke directly to his insatiable thirst for knowledge.

"It is in these rooms that I can learn, and it is here where I find inspiration."

He would use these precious moments in an empty classroom to take in the business models pinned up on the walls or the colourful infographics of vision and value statements, and he would sometimes pen down an inspirational message from the laminates of leadership. Like both a magnet and a sponge he would attract and retain this information, and it was clear that his mind was always working to mould it into something useful. Knowledge.

The accumulation of knowledge has always been considered a noble pursuit, and indeed, as parents, we invest heavily in that journey for our children. Later in our careers our employers may take over that responsibility, and if we are wise, like Humphrey, we will take it on ourselves. I have never seen a compelling argument against the lifelong benefits of continuous learning.

Mahatma Gandhi spoke about seven social, or even 'deadly' sins—the sort of things which might destroy Humanity from within. One of them was *Knowledge without Character.*

Whilst knowledge is infinite, perhaps character is less so, and if knowledge is what we gain, character may be what we choose to do with that knowledge. I guess in Gandhi's eyes it would be sinful to pursue knowledge without building the character to use that knowledge wisely. Or, indeed, sometimes not to use it at all.

We have all the knowledge on climate change but we lack the character to act. I know that exercise is good for me, but on a cold winter's morning, my character and its need for comfort keeps me wrapped in the warmth of my bed. My neighbour has first-hand knowledge that a visitor popped around under the guise of a delivery, and we shared a cold beer together during lock down. His character and the desire for a long-term relationship guided his judgement to let us be.

To keep informed during this pandemic, or any other crisis, is a choice to build one's knowledge base. To disseminate fake news like a student handing out flyers at a traffic light for a burger special on a Saturday morning is to erode one's character.

Humphrey, that trolley pushing gleaner of knowledge, once let slip that he loved to write poetry. I asked him if he would like to share any of his thoughts with me. He took a step further by asking if he could share his latest poem with our class. Which he did. Humphrey stepped out from behind his trolley, he closed his eyes and opened up his character.

Silent Tear

Just close your eyes and see,

All the memories that you have of me

Just sit and relax and you'll find,

That I'm sitting there inside your mind.

Don't cry for me now coz I'm gone

For where I am, I'm in the land of song

There's no pain, there's no fear there

So please dry away all those tears.

Don't think of me in the dark and cold

For where I am, I'm no longer getting old.

I'm in this place that's filled with love,

Known to you all as up above.

Don't stand and weep at my grave,

I'm not there...

There are things in life that we don't want anyone to know,

But someone must know.

Things we don't want them to happen,

But have to happen.

And people we can't leave without but soon have to let go...

Faith often shines brightest when life seems to be dark... *By Humphrey*

On a Friday afternoon, in front of a room full of learning leaders there was not a dry eye in the house and no amount of chocolate-covered sugar or sugar-coated mints could have induced a greater sense of alive engagement.

We were impressed by his knowledge, but we were floored by his character.

I guess in leadership, knowledge will earn you accolades, but character will find you followers.

I wonder if what I'm choosing to share, or sometimes choosing not to share, is helping me build my own character? It requires far more work to build and maintain the cathedral of character than it does to stock the warehouse of knowledge.

Fighting with Two Sticks

"Ukushaya Ngezinduku Ezimbili"

A dead and half plucked Pel's Fishing Owl hangs silently in the heat of the traditional healers' market in Warwick triangle in the centre of Durban. Even in death, it carries the regal air of a superior presence, and it remains top of the list of any ornithologists' must-see birds. People travel from all over the world to see this spectacular owl, but no birder ever wants to see one dead.

These Owls are best seen along the well wooded rivers of Southern Africa, and according to the Roberts Bird App, there are only three pairs of these 'whispering death' fishers along 4.8km of River in KwaZulu Natal. Other pairs are scattered through the Okavango Swamps of Botswana, along the Zambezi and through the Kruger National Park; but there are only three known pairs in KZN.

How does a seventh dead owl find its way into these markets?

Sadly, the owl is not alone. On this Saturday morning I see countless wild animals including three honey badger hides and a handful of pangolin scales. This shy and friendly animal is more persecuted by poaching than even the rhino, and I struggle to make sense of it all amid the emotions of sadness infused with anger.

I have never seen a pangolin alive in the wild, yet I have seen one dead in the markets.

Why, with modern medicine is there a need for this outdated belief system?

I have asked this question many times, and only recently did a phrase gifted to me by a colleague and friend stick in my mind long enough to be toyed with:

"Ukushaya ngezinduku ezimbili."

Fighting with two sticks.

There is a mixture of old culture and modern medicine at play here, and some distrust and scepticism exist at both ends of the spectrum. Stories and cures have been handed down from generation to generation and some may well have become lost in the smoky haze of fireside translation. Equally the corporate greed of some of the modern medicine makers make these remedies out of reach for so many of the sick and the dying, and anger festers in an unhealable wound. In the middle of this dichotomy exists a market of duality and when desperate people are in need of healing, they can cocoon into the comfort of cultural cures, or move mindfully into modern medicine.

They can fight with two sticks.

In the martial art of stick fighting, two sticks are used. The 'Isiquili' is the attacking stick and the 'Uboko' is the one used for defence.

A young fighter was left hopelessly vulnerable with only one stick, and for the first time something struck a chord in my own consciousness.

When I only have one single version of the truth, I am fighting with one stick.

With that stick I try to beat the pictures in my mind into submission. Pictures of superiority versus inferiority and pictures of a finite, linear world. I use my single stick to carve out silos of us being separate and disconnected, and if that is the only stick I have, I will drum it hard to produce power to get things done.

With only one stick, it is highly likely that I will see the world as a hostile and unfriendly place.

But if I pick up another stick, I can hold two conflicting viewpoints in my armoury. I can attack and defend.

No boxer ever won for too long in his career on all-out attack, and even the great Muhammed Ali had to learn how to absorb a few punches and avoid as many in defence as he could land in attack. Great rugby teams can do both, and they can turn one to the other in a snap moment of the bounce of an odd shaped ball.

Even Michael "Whispering Death" Holding himself, the great West Indian fast bowler, had more than one variety of delivery. Arguably the fastest bowler the world has ever seen, he would approach the crease with such fluidity and in complete silence, that the umpires couldn't hear him coming. Perhaps like the Pel's Fishing Owl he had extra feathers on his flight feathers to reduce turbulence and therefore sound. From there he could unleash a bouncer clocked at 156km/h or produce a slow ball which had the batsman playing his shot almost before he had taken guard.

Not easy to bat against a bowler who has two sticks.

Imagine facing Shane Warne who had all six known variations of leg spin, and could bowl them all with differing flight and speed. That is a whole quiver full of different sticks. No surprise he took a few of those in his time.

Michael Holding might not have been the best batsman around, but according to Wikipedia, he made a quarter of all his test runs in sixes and he still holds the highest tenth wicket partnership in an ODI during an unbroken stand of 106 with none other than the great Viv Richards. Now there's another example of the twin sticks of elegance and brute force.

And no helmet.

But back to the point. Or points?

Perhaps what I need to do is not so much to go out and look for new sticks, but rather to polish the ones I may already have?

Could I re-examine the pictures I hold in my head to see another side? That there may be many versions of the truth, and that life could be infinite at times? Might we be infinitely connected as opposed to separate and disconnected?

When I smile and someone smiles back, is that not evidence of the possibility of a friendly world?

Could we really embrace and celebrate our uniqueness instead of being mired in constant competition?

If you have ever been to Mahatma Gandhi's house in Inanda, KZN, that hotbed and melting pot of political thought and leadership, you will have seen a reference to what he referred to as "7 deadly sins".

"Wealth without Work

Pleasure without Conscience

Knowledge without Character

Commerce without Morality

Science without Humanity

Religion without Sacrifice

Politics without Principle."

Perhaps the world has tried to fight for too long armed only with the left-hand sticks?

We have been relentlessly and ruthlessly focused on wealth, pleasure, knowledge, commerce, science, religion, and politics.

Maybe a look through another lens will offer us redemption from the sins?

Work, conscience, character, morality, humanity, sacrifice, principle.

If we build these things, I guess in Gandhi's world, we live in less sin.

Baltes and Staudinger (2000), postulate that one of the five components of wisdom is the ability to hold different contexts of ambiguity in uncertainty.

I think that is called fighting with two sticks, and the wisdom to know when to use which.

Of course, I still far prefer to see a Pel's Fishing Owl in full flight, and not hanging half plucked with a dead eyed stare from the rafters of a tin stall, but maybe I'm learning to live a little more comfortably in the discomfort of conflicting viewpoints.

There had been a deluge of rain in KZN in the fortnight before our arrival for a Leading with Humanity week, and as a result there was an abundance of mud.

We learned through experience, that when you have only one set of wheels turning, your vehicle eventually nestles up to its chassis and becomes immovable in a hole of its own making. Sometimes we do exactly the same, and spinning the wheels of the same old tired story further entrenches us in the perceived succour of the place in which we were before.

I guess if you stick with one stick, you become stuck.

And we can't afford to remain stuck for too long in a fast-changing world.

POLARITY 2

IS THE WORLD A FINITE PLACE OR AN INFINITE PLACE?

The higher goal here is to encourage more generosity and sharing.

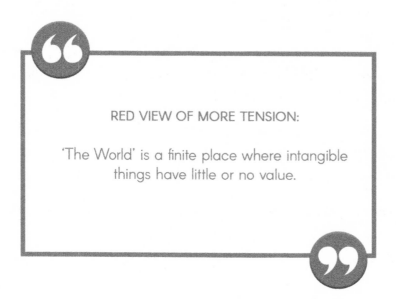

RED VIEW OF MORE TENSION:

'The World' is a finite place where intangible things have little or no value.

Please remember that this view is not wrong in isolation. There are many things which are finite and we should treat them with great stewardship. Our earth will all its Oceans and Rivers is not endless, and we should treat it with a mindset of sustainability. Money is finite, and I shouldn't waste it, and perhaps the most finite thing I have left on this Earth and in this life is my time, and yet I treat it sometimes as if it were an infinite concept. I will do the important things later, or when I retire, or when my pension kicks in.

However, If I lean too far to this side of the continuum, I will fight hard to grab my slice of the pie. I will pay attention only to those things which can be counted on a linear balance sheet or a CV of measurable achievements, and I may limit my life to the perceived certainties of boundaries.

The membership of the English alphabet is finite. There are twenty-six unique and measurable characters in its exclusive club.

The world of music has somewhere between 8 and 12 notes. My memory is hazy from too many smacks on the head with a recorder by my frustrated music teacher at school. Google tells me there are only twelve musical notes including the sharps.

All the colours around us are a combination of only three primary components. Let's add in the shades of black and white, and that makes five distinct and finite individuals.

Yet, it is the combinations of these finite components which lead to the infinite libraries of literature, endless new music, and photographs we haven't yet dreamed of admiring.

To see these magical outcomes, we will need to look through another set of lenses.

BLUE VIEW TOWARDS CONNECTION:

'The World' is an infinite place where intangible things carry great value.

If I 'SEE' this picture, my 'DO' will be to embrace the uncertain, and my 'GET' might result in more possibility and certainly more generosity.

In this chapter, we will count the apples in the seeds sown by an infinite player. We will meet young chess players whose lessons on life pour infinitely off the chess boards of their learning. A security guard shows the infinity of care, and an unwelcome immigrant might show immeasurable courage in saving your child. We will visit the hospital bed of one of the bravest young girls I know, and dance with a resilient dad in a different hospital parking lot. Let's stand on a rugby field as we watch a team inspired by a seemingly limitless belief in themselves and as we do, look at a different view of time which values the infinite quality of impact of the time we spend, over the finite amount of its quantity. Lastly in this chapter, we will see that there are far reaching consequences of sharing a simple biscuit.

"Not everything that counts can be counted, and not everything that can be counted counts."

Albert Einstein

Now there was an infinite thinker.

An Infinite Player

"You can count how many seeds are in the apple, but not how many apples are in the seed."

Ken Kesey

Ken Kesey was an American novelist and perhaps most famous for his book *One Flew Over the Cuckoo's Nest*, which was turned into a movie in which Jack Nicholson won an Oscar in 1976. If you watch that movie, you will know that the author must have seen life through a different lens, and he held an unconventional view of the world around him.

That simple yet profound quote speaks about a world of reality and a world of possibility. A world where the answer is right, and there is only one, versus a world which values the question more than the answer, even if it is right. There is an exact number to the first half of the quote and there is little room for argument and no need for auditing. There is no way of knowing the answer to the second half of that wonderful statement. In a linear, measurable and exact manner, a first-grade school goer will confidently give you the correct answer to the number of seeds in an apple. No quantum physicist would dare venture a definitive answer into the exponential thought of how many apples are in each seed because, well, because it depends.

That quote shows the difference between a finite world and an infinite world.

A large part of our world seems fixated on the finite. Measure, predict, drive for efficiencies, declare a winner, rank the top 100 school rugby teams over the last 10 years, beat everyone else, grab market share, win this quarters best performing asset manager prize, be the number one sales agent. Win the argument with your spouse. Always.

If the world is a finite place and only tangible things carry value, then you better fight to be number one. Grab your share of the pie and live by the mantra that second place is the first loser. Count the seeds in the apple.

But what if the view of the world was infinite? What if the intangibles like love and appreciation, hope and gratitude, friendship and trust were valued as much? And aren't those things immeasurable by nature, anyway? Do we rank our friends on a quarterly basis, can you express what one word of support means to a young sportsman, and what a few minutes of shut-up-and-be-silent-listening might do for a marriage? How many apples of possibility could grow from the seed of an idea well listened to, or a hug of compassion, or a small show of Humanity? Think about the potential of the apples in each seed.

In an extraordinarily well researched book called "No Contest", the author Alfie Kohn captures a stunning sentiment which argues against the popular view that competition always promotes excellence:

"Trying to do well and trying to beat others are two different things."

Trying to beat others. Finite. Trying to do well. Infinite.

I have already introduced you to my cousin Colin, the squash player, and his infinite outlook on life.

He imagined the apples in the seeds of relationships long after the finite doors of the squash results were closed.

Our lives are finite and there will be an end to them someday. I wonder if we could live them in an infinite way?

P.S. Ironically, but maybe so true of an infinite world, I received news of the passing of Ken Hovelmeier within minutes of finishing this reflection. In the world of squash, this man was nothing short of legendary. As a coach he was unparalleled, and he fined tuned many accomplished players into many a great one through his ability to listen. His hearing was so keen that he could decipher a well struck shot from a poor one and he could deduce the faint placing of footwork through his ear drum. He relied heavily on this sense because he was blind.

He saw nothing yet missed even less. He had no sight, but extraordinary vision. He took a finite disability and lived an infinitely meaningful life.

Hovvy, as he was affectionately known, rebuilt a Mini's engine, knew every member of staff by the way they walked down the corridors of Saints, and by the time any schoolboy had spent a few months in the College, he knew most of them by their voice.

He lives on in the infinity and in the legacy of memory.

RIP, Hovvy. As an infinite player you opened many eyes through your sense of Humanity.

P.P.S in the last 12 hours Our class WhatsApp group has been alive with stories of this man's influence. Our school days were finite, and they were over a long time ago. What we learned about ourselves, our relationships together, and the world around us lives on in a truly infinite way.

The world is both finite and infinite—it just seems there is more joy and significance in being an infinite player.

Chess Masters of Bhambayi

When Mumbai in India was still called Bombay, Bhambayi developed as a 'squatter camp' between Phoenix and Inanda in Kwa Zulu Natal, South Africa. It is a horrible phrase, 'squatter camp', but that is what it was called in those days, and even now, some decades after the dismantlement of Apartheid, the more appropriate and dignified term of 'informal settlement' should be rolling off the tongue with far more ease and grace than it does currently. Old habits die hard, and if we could look at an informal settlement as opposed to a squatter camp, or replace 'illegal immigrant' with 'undocumented worker', we might make progress if only through a new lens of compassion. We might fear living next door to a squatter camp with its perceived squalor, yet we spend money on second homes and flock down to coastal resorts for a more informal way of life. A large and powerful nation was swung on the negative perception of 'illegal immigrants', yet on the notice board of the local Spar in St Francis Bay in the Eastern Cape—an informal settlement for holiday makers if ever there was one—are no fewer than eight Malawian advertisements looking for work.

Undocumented or not, they will all find work before the December holidays in a few weeks; but perhaps that is the subject of another story.

I want to take you back to Bhambayi.

In the turbulence of the nineteen eighties, this settlement grew amidst the hotbed of political and religious leadership which has defined it for decades. Much of neighbouring Phoenix was damaged during the Inanda riots in 1985 including Gandhi's own house, Sarvodaya—'wellbeing for all' which was burned down but rebuilt and stands today as a monument to Mahatma, The Great One.

Due to the Indian influence of Gandhi's Phoenix, the area picked up its name as a colloquialism of Bhambayi, and 'Kasi taal'—the language of these locations—changed the colonialist tones of Bombay into new street maps long before Mumbai, India was born in 1995.

Gandhi's house and its peaceful surrounds is where we meet as a group to discuss the thoughts and experiences of the weekend, and this time there were a few new faces in the circle as some community members had joined us to tell their story. Gently driven by the most appropriately named young woman, Blessing, theirs is a story of emerging triumph. They work hard to figure out their own way out of some difficult circumstances, as they turn leadership theory into admirable action.

In the centre of the circle lie all the potions and lotions, pamphlets, plants and puff adder parts we have collected in an immersive quest for connection and understanding, and on the periphery of the same circle sit two young boys.

Two young boys and a chess board.

The boys are brothers, and the younger one who is not yet four years old, pulls each piece of the black and white armies of sixteen from the plastic packets they are wrapped in, and ceremoniously names each one as he correctly places them with great dignity on their designated square. He pays as much attention to each pawn as he does to the king, and there was Lesson One in leadership. No one is more important than any other, and just because the Queen can fly business class to all corners of the globe, a pawn can win you a game by sometimes just holding their ground.

I looked up at the photographs on the wall behind these chess players, and the faces beaming down on him were once considered mere pawns.

Mahatma Gandhi and his greatest teacher, his wife, Kasturba held their ground, and check mated the British Empire. With their Kings and their Queens.

From the moment the pieces were perfectly lined up, the game between the brothers was played in silence out of respect for the learning taking place in the circle of delegates. The learning however was not confined to the speaking, and our attention shifted to the unfolding of the theatre at play. For it was nothing short of theatrical.

The older brother, a few months short of ten years old, was immaculately dressed in his Sunday best. He wore a perfectly pressed grey suit with a black velvet lapel. The cuffs and collar of his pink shirt added some glorious colour to his attire, and the only thing brighter and shinier than his silky white tie, were his teeth.

As he taught his brother in silence, he smiled a lot. He clapped his hands without a sound in appreciative applause for every good move made, and when an obvious mistake was made, he pondered on it in the pose of Auguste Rodin's 'The Thinker'. Slowly, a loving frown might emerge with the sad face of a mime in an act of mummery of which even the magnificently mute Marcel Marceau would have been most proud.

There were more lessons right there. Appreciation and feedback are gifts given even in silence, and when the message comes not from words, but from the body, it is universal in its reach. Whilst the Finnish delegates in our circle would have been hard pressed to understand a Zulu translation of the lessons in chess, they could see a master teacher at work, simply through who he was being.

In their play of chess, we were learning the game of life. Actions taken today have far reaching consequences, so think wisely, but try not to become fixated on the detail. Be flexible. There is some debate as to what is more plentiful—the number of atoms in our observable universe, or the number of possible moves in a chess game? Either way, it is a big number, and a lot can change. A move backwards can be more important than a move forwards, and besides, the back row of the cinema is always a place of more possibility than the front. Every movie going teenager knows that.

While a bad move may be punished immediately, an opportunity missed may go unrewarded for a lifetime, and perhaps that is far more painful?

So, while these young men— 'Blessed' by the presence of their mother— played on, I could not stop the thoughts and questions in my own mind as they manifested themselves through my pen and onto the pages of my journal.

Who am I giving feedback to, and how am I giving it? Could I find the artful blend between strategy and patience as non-negotiable necessities in my life? Am I seeing the lessons in defeat as much as I am in victory, and treating these Kiplingesque 'imposters just the same?'

Do I know the rules of the game, make the most of the situation at hand, and just who or what is the king in my life which I am trying so hard to protect? Could I avoid the dreaded 'zugzwang'—a time when you are compelled to make a move which in some way or another is damaging or detrimental to one's position?

I am not sure if the Gandhi's ever played chess, but I am sure they would have approved of the lessons and these resulting questions.

The young brothers finished their chess game. It didn't seem to have a winner except in the learning of lessons themselves, and at the end of the exhibition, the king was wrapped up lovingly in the same manner and the same plastic bank packet as the pawn, and closed back in the box.

Another lesson right there in living a life of success, or significance. We all return to the same earth in some form or another.

I had been wrong about this young teacher's smile being the only thing brighter than his silky white scarf.

His eyes shone way brighter even than his teeth, and as he beamed his gratitude on departure, these sparkling portals to his soul highlighted that he was already a master.

If not yet in chess, certainly a master of his own destiny.

Courage and Care

Xolani Hlabisa is a security guard.

There is no boom by which he stands, or padlocked entrance. He has no glass fronted hut to sit behind with high tech cameras, and there are no telephone directory sized manuals of paper on which to sign. I have often wondered what happens to those reams of illegible scribbles which one finds at office blocks and housing estates? The cynic in me says they are sold to call centre sales agents, but if I've learned one thing from my time with Xolani, it is not to live with a cynical mindset.

Armed only with a torch and some old batteries, his calm presence and fading torchlight guide us around the open camp at night, and he is wide awake to the presence not of criminals, but of creatures—every kind of creature which a hugely diverse African wilderness could throw at one.

He speaks from the heart of his two young sons, and his home in KwaNibela close to Lake St Lucia, and one can imagine him exhibiting the same form of courageous protection towards his own family.

Here he carries out his duties with an old torch and even older batteries. I wonder how similarly under resourced he must be in looking after his two boys?

I wonder if such measurable resources, or lack of them ever hold him back? He has others in abundance.

Courage being just one.

The last time we were here, our colleague suffered a bloody nose. It was no ordinary bleed, as it went on for over 18 hours. In his stubborn Rhodesian bush war and farmland manner he was not too perturbed, and was more anxious in missing the evening's proceedings round the fire.

We were a lot more worried.

Xolani gently but firmly guided our wounded friend back to his tent, and popped in every half an hour that night to check in on the sleeping man.

It turns out that Xolani's real love is as a care giver. He practiced this for four years in Johannesburg, and is also an HIV-Aids Counsellor. I asked him where he thought this passion came from. He replied that he was just born with it. It is in his name.

Xolani means 'peace', or to be at peace, and he sees himself as a bringer of peace.

Perhaps his parents were onto something when they named him. They would be immensely proud of another of his immeasurable attributes:

Care.

Not a few weeks later, a news story hits the CNN headlines. A 22-year-old Malian immigrant on his way to a football match in Paris, France. (The News Channel makes this seemingly ridiculous differentiation because there are apparently around twenty-five places called Paris in the US, and we wouldn't want anyone from the flyover states to be confused— although they are probably watching Fox news anyway.) This illegal, and largely unwanted immigrant of a few months notices a commotion on the street. Hooters are honking and people are panicking. He looks up and there from four stories up on the ledge of an apartment block is a four-year-old child dangling from his fingertips.

Like a human Spiderman he ascends the front façade of the building. His physique is way stronger than his fear, and he is encouraged from the streets by loud chants of 'Allez, allez, allez." Balcony by balcony he jumps in a cross between PT and Parkour, and with seemingly effortless pull ups, he reaches his target and swings him to safety.

From street to sheet took thirty-six seconds.

Mamoudou Gassama met with French President Emmanuel Macron. He was granted French citizenship and a job as a Parisian fireman. An obvious occupation for a man who doesn't even need the ladders!

But this is not why he did what he did. He just loves children he said, and would not have wanted him to be hurt.

In a world trying hard to isolate itself, the mere mention of the word immigrant is enough to swing a national vote, and true heroes like this would be expelled and turned away at the borders. Marginalised back to the masses. People like that are not welcome here—send them back to where they belong. Aliens.

Perhaps the only thing 'Alien' about him was his exquisite blend of courage and care?

I wonder what the parents of the dangling toddler are thinking now with their son safely cocooned in the comfort of a fine Parisian percale?

Care does not just arrive because of an exorbitant medical aid, and courage has no need for capes. They arrive quietly and unexpectedly in the heat of the moment or in the dead of night.

They arrive to save your child.

Or to quietly check your pulse.

Could we show a little care in our courage, and Heaven knows it takes courage to show how much we care.

Bravery

There is apparently a difference between courage and bravery. According to the infinitely generous source of Wikipedia, it revolves around the presence or the absence of fear. Courage is action in the face of fear whilst bravery seems to be fearless action. To really understand the semantics for this reflection, I'd have to climb into the mind of an energetic Jack Russel which I doubt would be possible even for Cesar Millan, that most famous celebrity dog whisperer.

What I saw, whilst his half-sister from another litter was struggling in the slobbering jowls of a massive Rottweiler may well have been a mixture of both. But for now, I'll call it bravery.

A fair estimate of an adult Rottweiler comes in at fifty kilograms. It is a whole lot larger from ground level after being flattened by its charge, and I am not sure if I have experienced a tackle like that since my fifteen minutes of rugby playing days in the South African Air Force. With my air pods scattered on the sidewalk still playing the dulcet tones of the poet David White and my phone in the street gutter, it felt as though I had hooked into a marlin. The problem was that one of my Jack Russells was the bait, and the other one was straining at his leash in an attempt to rescue his sibling.

Having seemingly done enough damage to the first dog, this land predator picked his beef with the second, and hoovered him up by the base of the spine and started to shake it around like a rag doll. Thankfully between the dog walker and my largely ineffectual stance on my knees in the gutter, the dogs were separated. Two days later, the stitches are healing, and although the injustice of paying a vet bill for the damage caused by another's unrestrained dog is still present, at least the anger is slowly abating.

What remains clear though is the memory of bravery when a ten-kilogram Jack Russel tries to even attempt to distract a fifty-kilogram Rottweiler. Think Peter Steph du Toit coming round the blind side of a rugby scrum, and there in his direct path is your seven-year-old son prepared to take the hit. For that is the comparative differential in size.

As this whole ordeal unfolded in a matter of seconds which seemed like hours, I kept having a single thought. Two years ago, a young friend, then aged eleven, was horribly mauled by the same species of dog. The details of the attack are not important for this reflection, it is her recovery which captured our hearts. With too many stitches to count, let alone type, her first words as she woke were to her night nurse who was sitting at her bedside along with her parents.

"I am so sorry that I kept you awake."

Needless to say, the magic of this brave young girl wandered and weaved through the wards of Millpark Hospital, and in an instant, she had the full love and support of the entire staff. Medical records don't say whether this contributed to her healing, but her recovery was miraculous, and as the adrenaline wanes from my own ordeal, it is still replaced with tears of inspiration caused by a brave young soul more worried about someone's sleep than her own searing pain.

As I sit with my stitched-up dogs on my lap, in the warmth of our living room, I am watching a different fight break out in the so called "Land of the free, and the home of the brave."

Taking a knee in America has become a completely contrasting phrase today than from when the NFL quarterback Colin Kaepernick planted his patella in protest against police brutality and systemic racism during the playing of their national anthem nearly four years ago in August of 2016. His action was passive and peaceful.

The knee to the neck for nine minutes which killed George Floyd was needlessly violent and was beyond the boundaries of brutality.

If America is really going to be the "home of the brave", then they will need to be exactly that. They will need to understand the meaning of a home, and the qualities required to be brave.

Unless you have a Mike Tyson accent, there is a big difference between showing faith and showing your face. Anyone can stand in front of a church holding The Good book in their hand—albeit upside down; it takes real bravery for the same person to live the message of that book from his heart.

Whether fear is present or not, bravery and courage are actions taken from a deep and inspiring place.

A Jack Russel knows this. And so too does a remarkable young lady who never stopped smiling through all her stitches and surgeries.

I wonder if when history writes its report card on leadership, whether the leaders at the top of the class will be those who were brave in this moment?

I hope so.

(With thanks for the soul and the sparkle of Kate Chapman—keep smiling brave girl)

And indeed, to all the millions of people out there who smile through their sorrow, and tap dance through their trauma. Be Brave!

Resilience

I recently attended a webinar on resilience.

The host and facilitator, James, told a story of his grandmother which if it isn't already, should be turned into a book. It could easily be the female version of the story of Louis Zamperini from the book and movie, Unbroken. There were elements of real personal tragedy and blossoming of bloody-minded triumph, and in her story were all the ingredients of living meaningfully with resilience as a lifelong companion by her side.

It was clear that the apple hadn't fallen far from the family tree as the resilience gene has clearly found fertile ground in her Grandson James as he told his story and helped us grasp the meaning and importance of this trusty torch and wise walking stick which helps us walk through trying times.

We know all too well of the general mess the world is in right now, and perhaps more than ever we need to build the resilience from within to cope with the overbearing negativity around us. Perhaps though that is just the story I'm telling myself, and I can't change the clown show which is currently happening on the world's biggest stage. The Presidential debate between Trump the terrible and Biden the boring is everything except presidential.

And yet, if we are aware, we see colourful flowers pushing themselves through layers of dried and hardened mud as they show themselves to an appreciative world.

In amongst the dry drivel and hardened headlines of a CNN news report, I saw such a flower in the gaudiest of pants and even ruder coloured shoes dancing in a parking lot.

The story unfolds that Chuck Yielding from Fort Worth, Texas USA, arrives every Tuesday to dance for his son Aiden who is suffering from cancer in a hospital ward. Because of Covid restrictions, he is unable to visit his own son who is undergoing chemotherapy for leukaemia in Cook's children's hospital. Luckily a glass window into young Aiden's room doesn't care for the restrictions and he is able to watch his father perform some truly unique and original dance moves while passers-by stare in disbelief.

I am sure they would gaze in admiration if they knew the story behind his seemingly ridiculous routine.

Aiden says it cheers him up sometimes, and that he doesn't feel alone; his father finds meaning in the dancing, as he deals with his own grief in the story.

And right there are three great practices to build resilience.

Find the humour even in the darkest times.

Look for meaning in the everyday and every week. Especially on Tuesdays in a parking lot.

Know that you are not alone. Even when isolated from your own nearest and dearest.

I wonder who I would risk looking like a fool for?

And when I do, it will be the people who laugh with me and not at me who will be my tribe.

For the journey of resilience is not one easily undertaken alone.

The webinar ended with the extraordinary voice of Maya Angelou who asked:

"Can you be a rainbow in somebody else's cloud?"

There were more colours in Dad Chuck's pants than any rainbow I've seen, and the smile on his son's face through a seventh story window must have removed any clouds in that moment.

He is with his son every original step of the way.

Belief

Schoolboy rugby in Johannesburg has always been one of my favourite spectator experiences.

The crisp Highveld mornings are defrosted by a cup of hot coffee and later on fuelled by a bacon and egg roll or a juicy rib burger, and as the day warms up, so too does the atmosphere. Team after team run on with passion while their nervous parents watch on and pray silently into the clouds of the steaming beverages—not so much for a win, but at least an injury free game. The spectators of all ages and in various states of attire start to gravitate towards the main event, and it seems as though the younger they are, the less they wear. Young girls walk in gaggles of giggles blissfully unaware of the event, but completely focused on the players, while their Fathers become instant refereeing experts on the sides of the main field.

It's just as well that the person in charge has a whistle, else he wouldn't utter a word—let alone into a wheeled scrum.

The war cries begin and the cheerleaders whip the air in a passionate plea for voluminous voices. The game begins. It is played. It ends.

There are handshakes and hugs afterwards—even if the odd handbag is thrown.

Since my own son has just started at this school, and has enjoyed his first season of College rugby, I have been a keen observer of the spirit and energy of the various teams, and even from the back row of rib burger braaiing, and I burned a few on Burger Field while watching, I have been held captivated by one team in particular. In a way, I wish it was some team less clichéd than the First XV. But it wasn't.

I watched infinitely talented teams lose more games because of the mistakes made from their mouths than their muscles, and I saw some teams win games with half their first picks in the sick bay. Gruelling game after magical match, however, I watched as one team took heed of their supporter's chant as another kick soared through the uprights from their mercurial fly half:

"I believe."

And as they believed, so too did the players, and so too did the crowd.

There were not many games that 'The Blues' played where they started comfortably in the lead. Most games I remember were an inspired comeback, and although this was no unbeaten season, something far more valuable was at play here.

Occasionally beaten but never bowed.

There was a courage in this team and a grit which was admirable. They played the sort of rugby one would be happy to pay money for to watch, and they played for each other. I don't remember any front row opposition being smaller in stature, and not once did our hooker pack down against a lighter counterpart. But not once was their heart any bigger than his.

A small blanket could have covered our entire forward pack as they moved into a counter shove at the breakdown, lineouts were stolen not just through height, but through the power and timing of the lift, and when the only regular Grade 11 in the pack has a work rate which is exhausting just to watch, something special happens.

Not once did our scrumhalf fail to get up again after being manhandled by men twice his size, and when the backline started to move, it was both mesmerising and magical. From deep inside our own 22-yard line there was a hunger to run and to run hard, and there has been a season full of electrifying moments and memories. When substitutes were required, they seemed to wear the same pride with the newly donned jersey. Crunching tackles (which drew almost more admiration from an adoring audience of adolescents) were made with every available sinew of strength and much slower paced wingers found a way over both the advantage line and the try line.

In a world short of belief, you young men seemed to have it in abundance, and although a great rugby season is not something which will earn accolades on a CV, the ingredients of a great season are not too different to those which will stand you all in good stead for the rest of your lives.

Respect. Passion. Pride. Determination. Courage. Care. These things are infinite.

And so too is belief.

Although you have been well led, you have also led yourselves and while you outplayed many teams this year, mostly you out-believed them.

I remain a proud old boy of one of those schools, but Thank You all for making me a very proud parent of this one.

A Proudly SJC Parent

P.S. Manuel de la Santos, a former Baseball player, and now one-legged golfer who says he has found his second leg on the golf course and has never been happier, has found this ingredient called belief.

Captain Tom Moore who will be 100 years old in 5 days' time has also unearthed this extraordinary energy which lies in believing. To date he has raised 28 million Pounds Sterling and has two entries in the Guinness Book of World Records.

He will 'Never walk alone' and perhaps he reminds us it is not necessarily that seeing is believing. Perhaps Believing is seeing. 25 April 2020

KAIROS

The Ancient Greeks often found many ways to describe a concept. In the English language for example we only have one word for love. We can love ice cream, rugby, sunsets, our family, reading, golf…whatever.

The Ancient Greeks had different words to describe facets of this concept— the love you have for your friend (Philia) is different to the love you have for your family and even mother-in-law (Storge). The erotic love you have for your partner (Eros) is going to show up differently for the unconditional love you might show to your children (Agape).

In no way is this reflection meant to be a lesson in Ancient Greek, but it serves to add both colour and depth to our understanding of the concept of love.

The same is true though in the concept of time. In English we have a linear, measurable understanding of time as a finite concept, and we call it chronological time. This apparently found its Ancient Greek roots in the word "CHRONOS".

Where there are always sixty seconds in a minute and sixty minutes in an hour and twenty-four hours in the day. It is linear, finite and measurable.

"KAIROS" is best defined as the moment when the minute of sixty seconds becomes a moment. Where the clock stops, time stands still for a while and the value lies not in the quantity of time, but on the impact of that time, and the relationship you had with someone or something in that moment.

It seems as though chronos moves past from one minute to the next, but Kairos lasts for AEONS, a third concept of time from the Ancient Greeks' meaning 'broad sweeps of time'.

I found a wonderful piece of writing describing how 'Kairos' time fits in with the picture of an infinite world.

"The action in a universe of possibility may be characterised as generative, or giving, in all senses of that word—producing new life, creating new ideas, consciously endowing with meaning, contributing, yielding to the power of contexts. The relationship *between* people and environments is highlighted, not the people and things themselves. Emotions that are often relegated to the special category of spirituality are abundant here: joy, grace, awe, wholeness, passion and compassion."

"There are moments in everyone's life when an experience of integration with the world transcends the business of survival—like seeing a grandchild for the first time, witnessing an Olympic record broken or the uncommon bravery of an ordinary citizen. For many, the experience of attending the dismantling of the Berlin Wall or of witnessing the emergence of Nelson Mandela from twenty-seven years of imprisonment may have been such a moment. Some find admission to the realm of possibility at a religious gathering, some in meditation, some by listening to great music. Often people enter this state in the presence of natural beauty or at the sight of something of infinite magnitude, an expanse of ocean or a towering sky. These are moments when we forget our*selves* and seem to become part of all being."

From *the Art of Possibility—Transforming Professional and Personal Life* by Rosamunde Stone Zander and Benjamin Zander

So, Kairos is not the twenty minutes I spend playing cricket in the garage, it is the value of the relationship we build in the process. Kairos is the one great thought in a two hour Zoom meeting which elevates the energy and the sense of possibility in the team. Kairos is not the hour long walk we might enjoy at the end of lockdown, it might be that moment of freedom we experience, or the greeting from a neighbour we haven't seen for weeks.

The greeting might only last for a few measurable seconds, but the impact of the greeting might last for years.

William Blake wrote about this concept beautifully, and although he didn't call it Kairos, I think the Ancient Greeks would be nodding in sage agreement:

"To see the world in a grain of sand,

And Heaven in a wild flower

To hold infinity in the palm of your hand

And eternity in an hour."

Even though it may be more difficult in times of lockdown I wonder if there aren't an abundance of these Kairos moments all around me.

A moment where I can notice a bird at the birdfeeder; where I can love my dogs, savour something special with my wife at the end of the day, watch a romcom with my daughter…

… and survive some brutal garage cricket with my son!

What is a Kairos moment which you have enjoyed today?

And what might be one you look forward to tomorrow?

When a Biscuit Is Shared

There seems to be a tension in our world at this moment where cautious optimism is losing its lustre. Dinner parties are dishing up depression and menus offer up a range of mass negativity. Smorgasbords of selfishness and buffets of buffoonery abound. There is more talk around packing for Portugal and emigrating to Euros than there is around a sensational Springbok victory over New Zealand at Ellis Park last weekend. And there is good reason for this.

One read through of the Sunday Times newspaper should give the average person enough incentive to buy a coffin before there is no more wood left to make them, give everything to your children, because that's really why we want to have the escape plan in place anyway—for the children, and move in to a permanent piece of real estate six feet under.

There are a few people for whom this would be a great option. It would save all the hassle of life between now and the ever after, and they could contribute by being the organic food which new vegetable gardens could thrive on. Though the bitterness of their human sentiment may even be too much for the broccoli to bear.

I'm being more than a little unfair. It is what happens when we live too long in a negative place. We become the negativity we hate hearing about. When all we ever see and hear is RED behaviour, we become RED ourselves and it becomes more difficult to make BLUE choices. More difficult, but not impossible.

There is an aggressive race as to what exactly is causing a downward spiral. Ebola continues to spread exponentially, and if ever there was evidence of us living in a connected world, this virus is making us aware of that. The rise of the Islamic State and its ruthless barbarism is the human equivalent of that unwanted illness. From Nkandla to nuclear agreements, Ukraine to U-boats, Sascoc to Shrien Dewani, there is a shade cloth of secrecy, a glut of greed and a clandestine conspiracy of corruption. Even the change rooms of the English Cricket Board, the supposed stronghold of statesmanship and domain of dignified decency has descended into a dangerous den. There is much to be RED about, which is why seeing another angle feels akin to observing the flowering of a desert plant.

We were enjoying an early breakfast meeting at the Mugg and Bean in Woodmead, and were delighted to be sitting safely and on time with a generous cappuccino. The traffic into town would give thousands of motorists another reason to apply for foreign passports due to an overturned vehicle on the Highway just off Grayston Drive.

On leaving, we gathered up the delicious but completely anti-Tim Noakes biscuits from the saucers of our completed coffees, and gave them—along with a cash tip to Patrick, the smiling car guard. His smile alone was worth a photograph, but it was nothing compared to our smiles when he promptly walked over and gave the second biscuit to his colleague. It had an immediate positive effect, and forthwith a second gratuity was handed over to the colleague to emphasise that such gracious sharing should be handsomely rewarded.

This RED world of ours is crying out for leadership, and we are anxious in its absence. Yet there it was right in front of us for all who cared to see it. It will not make the Sunday headlines, and it will not change policies around energy or education, but if leadership is about giving, then we saw it starkly even in the form of a simple shared snack.

What can our leaders give us to allay our angst, filter our fears and prevent us from packing for Portugal?

Just a little more.

A little more openness and honesty, accountability and action, care and concern, and—at the very least—a feeling of hope that if we as the taxpayers give you two biscuits, you will at least give one of them to a worthy cause and not hoard them both with a tenderised clause to claim a third, as yet unmade, biscuit.

Like Patrick the generous car guard, I too may not be able to impact on the loudest or most silent of political personas, with all their masks and mouthpieces, but I know that I could be more giving. Especially of the things that really count. Love and the ability to listen, Time and truth and trust and energy with all my enthusiasm.

Leadership only demands of us that which we are capable to give. Those are simple things, and if I can't give them then I'm not leading.

Never again will I leave a biscuit on my saucer.

It can be that simple sometimes.

POLARITY 3

IS THE WORLD A FRIENDLY OR AN UNFRIENDLY PLACE?

The higher goal here is to understand relationship.

RED VIEW OF MORE TENSION:

'The World' is an unfriendly place.

This is true. The world is unfriendly at times. Unfriendly and unfair. There are wars and famines, wild fires and filth. There is still poverty and persecution, anger and abuse, corruption and cruelty. We can't escape this side of the polarity, and being aware of these possible dangers and deceits is a huge part of the responsibility I carry as a parent.

But it is not the full picture.

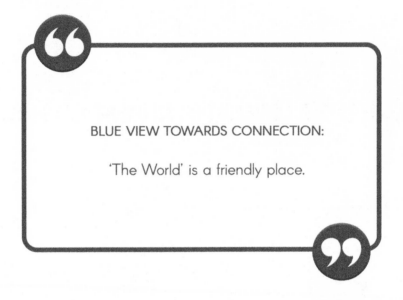

BLUE VIEW TOWARDS CONNECTION:

'The World' is a friendly place.

When I look through this lens, I can approach with a greeting. I can start a conversation and the 'GET' is relationship.

In the stories of this chapter, we will meet the only man in history to have competed in track and field in six consecutive Olympic Games, and the greeting which started that relationship. We will see the possibility of a friendly outcome emerge from a seemingly unfriendly situation. We will meet some friendly lock pickers who offer their help, and meet both humans and elephant herds who find friendliness in protecting each other's hearts. In the heat of an unfriendly fire, we will encounter the hearts of friendly firefighters, and we will enjoy a haircut from the other side of a busy road. We will hear the soothing tones of piano keys being played through a catastrophe, and that at all times if we are to see the joy in relationship, it pays to be kind.

"Relationships are all there is."

Margaret Wheatley

Think of someone who makes your world a friendly place. Phone them if you can, but thank them, regardless.

Our Heroes Are Already Here

I was thankful for the air conditioning. And the meal. A five star, all you can eat English breakfast with bottomless coffee.

The dining room was full today, even more so than my plate was and my stomach was about to be. It was the first time I had seen people looking for a place to sit in this hotel breakfast room, and I wondered why this was so on this Saturday morning in Luanda, Angola.

Normally there was a table or two of American oil company executives, or a small conference delegation, but today it was different. As I observed from behind my stack of sausages, and a barricade of bacon, I noticed that there was a peculiar similarity to the patrons around the buffet, and as I followed one with my eyes to a table of ten, it was immediately obvious that their entire body fat percentages added up would still be less than mine, and that I had more calories on a single plate than they had on their table.

They were all wearing athletic gear and bright running shoes, and I thought how strange it was that the local running club would meet at an expensive hotel to eat salad or a sliver of melon for breakfast.

A neatly dressed man walked past with a side plate of fruit. He was not in his running kit but was still eating in the same sparse manner of his fellow diners, and it was clear that he was looking for a place to sit. I managed to swallow a healthy mouthful of eggs before I greeted him and asked if he would like to sit at my table for two. Besides, I was looking forward to understanding what was at the heart of this strange gathering of exercisers.

He graciously accepted. And so, my learning started.

This was a gathering of the world's great half marathon runners to run the inaugural Luanda Half Marathon. He pointed out a number of household names, and as he did so, I berated myself for not recognising some of them. I also started to wish that I'd taken a bit more fruit and a lot less fat.

As we talked, people young and old walked past to greet him, some asked him to sign his autograph and others politely popped in for a selfie. All of them walked away with a smile and a lightness in their step. As if they needed that.

My intrigue was piqued when the organiser of the event pulled up a chair, and said to me how lucky I was to be sitting at this man's table.

I was sitting with an Olympian, he said excitedly.

We talked some more, swapped business cards, took the obligatory picture, exchanged pleasantries and I left in a masked hurry. No, not to the gents, but rather straight to Google.

João N'Tyamba was born in 1968 in Lubango, Angola.

He is the only man in history to have competed in track and field in Six Olympic Games. There have been others in Equestrian and shooting and sailing who have competed in more, but as a true athlete, he is the only man to have achieved this.

Four women have achieved this by the way, but that is a subject for another essay. I have long held the belief that the world is crying out for more of their leadership. Perhaps now more than ever.

João N'Tyamba, at the time of writing, was also the Angolan record holder in the 800m, 1000m, 1500m, 3000m, 10 000m, Half Marathon and Full Marathon.

He never won a medal in twenty years of top-level competition which included five world championships, but imagine just competing at that level for over two decades, and having the ability and agility to adapt to different distances over his career.

He competed in his first Olympic Games in Seoul in 1988, and ran his last one in Beijing in 2008, all the while running for his country.

In 1988 I was in my first year in the South African Airforce, supporting a war against that same country.

I learned a lot more than just athletics during that remarkable and spontaneous breakfast.

It started with a simple greeting and a warm acceptance. It led to a conversation over a meal. It remains to this day as one of the great pieces of understanding about myself and others.

I wonder if the world may just need to eat together a little more?

We often cry out that Africa needs more heroes. People like João who have both honour and humility, hospitality and humanity.

Perhaps Africa has plenty.

We may just need to notice them?

Kites, Fires and an Interesting Visitor

It is not often when one is mesmerised by the sight of a black plastic bag. In fact, most often they are repulsive sights, strewn across strands of rural and urban wire fences like dirty debris dumped without care. Or half chewed by desperate dogs who leave the contents to stink in the sun, like a lion leaves the stomach contents of its kill.

The objects of my transfixed gaze were not attached to any earthly structure flapping around like an old defeated flag. Instead, they were flying, and flying amazingly high, attached only to the joy of a child's fingertip through a gossamer like strand of silk. These were well crafted kites. Light enough to fly high over the RDP houses of Kwa Mashu, but strong enough to withstand the strong breeze of an impending storm. They were perfectly balanced, and even had a knotted tail which weaved and danced through the darkening winds.

Of course, there was much I'd like to emulate in my own life in the observing of those kites. Strength with flexibility. Absorption and agility. The simple pleasure of flying a kite.

What really struck me though was the ingenuity, and I realised maybe for the first time why the word 'genius' lies at the heart of ingenuity. Someone with genius crafted those kites, and I wondered whether my children, with all their private school education could ever come close. I know I couldn't.

Could we find such simple pleasure in a black plastic bag, when it seems that today only the latest technology, camping accessory or Ping G20 driver can hold our attention and our affection for a mere modicum of minutes?

In Havelock, an old woman, broad as she was tall, taught me a valuable lesson in leadership.

With a slow and steady gait and barely able to pass through the narrow passages of the organic structure of the informal settlement, her whole being stopped as she noticed the wisp of smoke, as thin as the Kwa Mashu kite's umbilical cords, rise from the inside of a locked shack.

In an instant there was action as the web of her network and the work of her influence took hold. The door was smashed open, the fire was isolated and water was brought. Who knows how long it may have taken to erupt in a full-blown shack fire, but the consequences of that are too disastrous to contemplate, especially given the little which people do have in these areas?

She knew what to do even in the full face of uncertainty, and she displayed all the skills of a true tracker in her awareness, decision making, and ability to influence others.

Leadership comes in multiple shapes and forms.

So, too, does courage.

And just when we think these forms belong only to the human realm of wisdom, we are joined on a game drive by a most unusual guest.

As we drove off the plains of Zuca in Phinda Game Reserve, and ambled our way up a chilly winter morning's dirt road, a reptilian head emerged from a burrow on the side of the road. Something scared it enough to leave the safety of its abode, and in its panic to dive back in at the sight of the noisy four tyred monolith, the rock monitor found that the way in was more challenging than the way out.

I have often found that in my own life.

It was as exposed and vulnerable in the open as a fledgling bird fallen from its own nest. In amongst the four deadly legs of metal and rubber— capable of crushing creatures many times larger than itself, with grinding gears and spinning scythes, and a plume of toxic gas from its tail —the monitor had choice, and it immediately chose an interesting course of action.

It chose to go in. It did not run away. It went right in to the heart of the beast, deep into its bodywork with all its grinding and gassing, cutting and crunching and crushing, all its heat and its hate.

When last did I ever do that? When did I seek safety in the very thing which scares me near to death and has had me running for the hills away from exposure and vulnerability and far away from the perceived failures of the day?

When did I see a friendly possibility past the perception of an unfriendly world?

Sometimes, I am learning that I have to go in. I have to go in to my roots. I have to dig deep to reach them. And I certainly have to go into my challenges to search for their root causes, to have the courage to dwell there for a while, and the resilience and energy to emerge with a different viewpoint and an exciting set of possibilities.

I knew all this once as I pulled off my first proper tackle on a rugby field, and it was an extraordinary reminder from the most unlikely of Lizards.

That large lizard like crusader would emerge from the chassis of its own chagrin, annoyed but alive, embarrassed but empowered, and faced not only with new possibilities, but a whole new territory many miles away from its previous one after its unintended Uber odyssey.

In his book "The Structure of Morale", JT Mac Curdy, a Canadian psychologist wrote this:

"We are all of us not merely liable to fear, we are also prone to be afraid of being afraid, and the conquering of fear produces exhilaration...When we have been afraid, that we may panic in an air raid, and, when it has happened, we have exhibited to others the calm exterior that we are now safe, the contrast between the previous apprehension and the present feeling of relief and feeling of security promotes a self-confidence that is the very Father and Mother of Courage."

How indeed do I build self-confidence if I don't understand self?

How do I build courage if I don't go in and face up to fear?

I don't need to buy a kite to enjoy one, and I can put out my own fires if I am prepared to move closer to the flame.

I can emerge from danger by going through it sometimes.

I've done this before; just ask that under-13 B rugby wing from Randburg Hoërskool!

I can do it again, and I can see friendliness in an unfriendly world.

Help Arrives in Many Different Forms

Africa is not for sissies.

This seems to be a well-known rallying cry when things go awry in a continent of contrasts. A continent as inconsistent as it is uncertain yet as surprising as it is spontaneous. South Africa is home to many of the toughest places on offer, and at the bottom of the alphabet but high up in the pecking order of uncompromising harshness lies the town of Zeerust.

In the 1980s, when South Africa was still engaged in two separate yet simultaneous wars, fresh conscripts prayed for navy or air force call ups, but would settle for anything except Zeerust. Oudtshoorn and Zeerust. These were places to be avoided at all costs. Two years of National Service in either of these desolate infantry bases would seem like a lifetime of hell. Indeed, for many they were.

As a loadmaster working at Waterkloof air force base, I remember well the different troops and their equipment being loaded to places like Rundu, Mpacha and Ondangwa—and if there are certain groups I remember, there is one group I could never forget. 32 Battalion, pronounced three-two, were described often as Apartheid South Africa's foreign legion, but the look in their eyes unveiled an experience far more sinister than that. They had seen some stuff for real which movies still dream of in make believe. There was a chiselled steeliness to their stare and their stance and one wouldn't dare mess with this elite force or their bags. Their luggage would be treated like gold and correctly labelled and loaded to their desired destination—an outcome rarely achieved in a largely disengaged defence force.

The point of this seemingly arbitrary rambling of a rankless troop is that the remnants of that feared fighting force of 'Three-two' now makes up the bulk of Two South African Infantry (2SAI) in Zeerust. I guess if you have already seen Hell, Zeerust must seem like a resting place as it was for Casper Hendrik Coetzee after whom Zee's Rust was named at his passing in the early eighteen sixties. One could easily be forgiven for thinking that the name of Zeerust must have something to do with its constant coating of red sand and rusty outlook, and indeed the local Tswana people here refer to it as 'Sefatlhane'—the place of dust.

Hard places have hard people, and in the parking lot outside the local Clicks pharmacy was one of its sons wrestling a piece of wire through the upturned passenger door latch of an old Toyota bakkie. I would love to have described this vehicle in full, but the only way that I knew it was a Toyota was through the extra layer of red dust on the back which made the writing stand out. Apart from that it was almost unrecognisable.

The wire wrestler though was dust free as the sweat from his exertions washed away the static sediment in rivulets of red. Even in August, the midday sun can push a bead in these parts, and as the temperature increased, so too did the intensity of the language. I can't pretend I had to cover my eleven-year-old son's ears, as sadly he has heard some of these profanities from his own father's frustrations—especially at television referees before, however there was a different gravelly roughness off the vocal cords of someone having grown up in a place where the air is as earthy as the ground which supplies it.

His 'Rogue' hat was wet around the seams and a new level of white salt ring was being formed from his labour. The two tone Senqu safari top was a soggy three tone by now, and the Johnson workforce trousers were hitched up to above his safety boot laces. The veins in his forearms looked as strained as the sinuous steel of the twisted wire, and even the ends of his long thin hair became matted from the sweat of his brow.

It was probably not a good time to give advice, and the look on his face when I quietly provided it confirmed that suspicion. It was then for the first time that I saw the gap in his teeth and thought he might devour my son like a mielie in this corner of the maize triangle. I pulled him a little closer so as to hide behind him, and the car cracker continued with a sniff and a snort that he had done this before as his mother had once again locked the keys in the car. It was then also for the first time I saw a touch of his Humanity. He was doing this for someone else—even if it was for his mother.

From the popular Wimpy, a fast-food eatery nearby, emerged a totally different energy.

Three young ladies in skin tight jeans and impossibly small stilettos sauntered slowly out of the fast-food style restaurant. Their made-up lips were still smacking at the last remnants of their meal, and the midday dusty silence was no more. They looked out of place, but seemed comfortable that the world was their oyster, and had a carefree holiday kind of an attitude. Time was on their side, and in no observable rush they walked abreast with no space for a fire hydrant bolted onto the wall of the covered mall walkway.

On seeing the sweating steelworker, the volume increased, but the pace remained constant.

"Haai, Boetie (Brother), let me show you."

Out of respect, this was phrased as a question; but it was quite clearly an instruction and there was no semblance of resistance offered as she gently took the well-used wire and reinserted it down the side of the window and into the rubber guard just above the locking mechanism.

In less than a change of traffic lights, of which there are three in this town, the door sprung open almost as wide as the bearded jaw of the Khaki clad man who tenderly held the helpers appropriately large take-out drink. He held onto that drink as his last refuge against an ego which had disappeared into the depths of a dusty doorframe.

He hardly had time to say Thank You, before she wobbled off with her friends without seemingly a break in their conversation. All I could glean from her in this potential library of information was that she was from Pretoria. I would have loved to have known more about where she learned this skill of lock picking and what else she did, or if this was more of a full-time pastime, but the moment had passed, and the rest remains guesswork.

I am guessing too that the grateful man with a new, yet unexpected access to his mother's vehicle had spent some time in the military here. He certainly looked the part, and if he had, he'd do well to heed the message in the motto of 2SAI Motorised Infantry in Zeerust:

"In Utrumque Paratus"—Prepared for all situations.

In this volatile, uncertain, complex and ambiguous world of the acronym VUCA, itself derived from military operations in the nineteen nineties, I wonder if we can ever be prepared for all situations?

But what I did learn is that friendly help can arrive in many unexpected shapes and forms, and I should be prepared to accept it when it comes.

I will also double check my car on the streets of Pretoria, though that might be looking through the lens of an unfriendly world.

Protect Each Other's Hearts

The ghost grey giant seemed to appear from nowhere. It started with one, and then we were surrounded. They were everywhere.

It didn't seem possible that the world's largest creature to have walked this earth in the last few million years could step so silently through the drought stricken broad leafed woodlands of Northern Kwa Zulu Natal. As one appeared, so did another, then another, until we were firmly in the firing line of a fast-moving breeding herd of these magnificent mammals. We gave them a respectful space and they veered off East, eyeballing us through a fine film of dust kicked up by their stiff legged shuffle. They seemed content as some sort of unwritten contract of trust between their security and our silence had been established.

The situation changed when their path was impeded once more by the presence of two construction vehicles filled with worried looking workers.

With every closing metre, the worry turned to fear and an already packed bunch huddled even closer for protection.

For some time in my life, I studied human energy. I strongly believed that energy is infectious—virally infectious; both positively and negatively. Perhaps until that moment, I had thought that this might be purely a human construct. But what I saw in the next few minutes helped me to understand that energy knows no boundaries.

As the panic permeated the hustling herd, their behaviour changed visibly in front of our eyes, and it mirrored that which altered their demeanour. Tension turned to trumpeting and trepidation, and the young elephant calves almost disappeared amongst their mothers' enveloping ears and tactile trunks. Those trunks equally capable of a caring caress and yet completely equipped to kill.

Separated by nothing more than an uneasy air and a set of flickering hazard lights, both the breeding herd and the workers hugged closer together. Each one triggering off a more terrified response in the other.

Perhaps they were close for a reason. Perhaps they were protecting each other's hearts.

This was a concept which would crop up many times during our week together, and a raft of reflections would emerge around this phrase:

"Protect each other's hearts."

Could I still give candid feedback to those I love, and yet still protect their hearts? Might I be able to allow my children to venture into a void of their own vulnerability, and just be there to protect their hearts which could build even bigger through every breakage?

Could I consider the hearts of others who I sometimes walk straight past, or carry a media fuelled perception of some unfounded kind of unworthiness?

Could I protect my own heart in the turmoil of constant comparison and endless evaluation?

And whose hearts could I reach out to each other's help me during life's inevitable struggles?

There is an African saying which reminds us that:

"In Africa, if you want to go fast, go alone, but if you want to go far, go together."

And as we grouped together on that last morning, perhaps we too were huddled close. United as a group who had shared an extraordinary experience, and maybe feeling a touch vulnerable at the thought of the threats of the other world into which we would be leading.

In that other world, just as in this one, we could do worse than simply being mindful of that caring commandment.

"Protect each other's hearts."

As we left in deep thought and decluttered contemplation, we knew this would be practiced by at least two men, coming from completely different walks of life, yet leaving as true friends.

They would be protecting each other's hearts.

Even with their own.

(With gratitude to Helgaard who shared this as a family value far too valuable to be kept from the world.)

Firefighters of St Francis

This village of St Francis Bay, has been shot in this movie before. Too many times already, and no doubt it will happen again. The unique quaintness of this Eastern Cape haven with its white walls and traditional thatch roofs carries a heavy price tag when mixed with a gale force westerly wind, a water scarce area and an errant cigarette, or braai coal, or naughty children, or arsonists malevolence, or pre-election campaign for a political land grab. The causes of the fire spin out of control in the coffee shops and on the beaches in a runaway rumour mill almost as wild as the fire itself. Stories flare up from the embers of suspicion and are fanned by sensationalism as the news spreads faster than the flames can find the next bed of thatch to devour in their relentless pursuit for the sea.

It seems even the fire wanted to cool down on this hot day.

Whilst narrow escapes, and the number of houses destroyed become the stuff of legend, and are spoken about over throat lozenging lagers at the local pub of the same name, one thing remains unbowed.

Community.

Whilst a squabble continues to surface, and a spat hisses and spits about the spit, in the midst of bickering on the beaches and rows over the roads, there were hotter topics to be dealt with today. A voluntary army emerged, a ramshackle squadron of men, women and children, of businessmen and bystanders, home owners and holiday makers, young and old, black, white and every shade in between fought a common enemy. Those closest to the frontline of the fury would emerge fairly close to the same soot covered hue anyway, and it struck me that in times of crisis we often forget our individual differences and instead embrace the collective. Why is it that you can wait many weeks for the delivery of a lounge suite from only an hour's drive away when at the mere sight of smoke, we can evacuate multiple households?

Maybe it boils down to meaning and purpose.

Thatch pullers pulled, roof wetters doused, bush clearers chopped and bakkies—a generic term for almost any vehicle with an open back, were loaded. The Spar provided water and cokes and no doubt many other things as did so many others. Farmers from as far as Oyster Bay teamed up with golf course staff to bring bowsers of water. People opened their homes.

And their hearts.

No one wants to see this sight. A catastrophic Catherine wheel of chaos. A fire fuelled fury of destruction which leaps and laughs and leaves eleven homes looking like they've been in a middle eastern war zone. At least that's the number I have heard reported—not the twenty-five, or the whole village, as some might have believed in the confusion of the inferno. No one wants to remember the smell of that appalling stench of smoke, or relive the touch of those taunting and teasing torch like tongues which curl and coil like cobras as they strike and spit and seethe. We'd all far rather remember the 'snap, crackle and pop' of a breakfast cereal of Rice Crispies, than recall the sounds of popping windows, crackling thatch and snapping safety relief valves of the gas bottles.

What we would do well to remember is the spirit of Humanity. The unselfish acts of everyday people and the heroism of people in the moment. The bravery of souls who help those they've never met, and possibly never will. The unconditional care of volunteers who removed everything from beloved pets to expensive motor cars away from the pyro path and off to safer havens.

This Bay will return to its haven like status. It has done so before. It will bounce back a little stronger maybe, and even a little wiser. Perhaps the bickering will continue, but hopefully with a different sense of community, and a little more compassion.

Sometimes we forget that we live in a heavenly place, but when Hell visits for a day we can all display the qualities of Saints and behave like Angels.

Imagine the country we should have. We have been in Hell before, and some say we are pretty close once more, but we have all the ingredients we need to pull back together from the brink.

Just remember the firefighters of St Francis. And then ask those they helped.

HAIRCUT

It's a day for a haircut. It's hot, it's muggy and I'm feeling particularly bothered and sweaty. I'm waiting impatiently for my combi window to be repaired, thanks to an inquisitive bargain hunter, and I need a break—a breath of fresh air. Often times I've considered a haircut to be an excuse for a relaxing break, a chance to take a breath and enjoy what is always for me a new fresh breath of life.

It's a time to think, from a comfortable chair in which you're expected to stay for the entire procedure—have your scalp massaged by soft skin and your hair ruffled by effeminate hands. No movement, no decisions, just a state between casual consciousness and drifting dreamland, and an excited anticipation as to what I might look like after this painless cosmetic surgery.

A change in looks often leads to a change in attitude—and I need one of those, so I go for a serious haircut.

I walk across from the window repairers to the Big Ben shopping centre. What used to be a clean and clinical little shopping centre with a bookstore and an expensive family restaurant and a marginalised black presence, as was so typical of the Apartheid 80's, has now become a colourful explosion of fruit sellers, some hand craft, cheap caravan take-aways, litter and jumble sales, with a constant stream of the multi-billion Rand business of buses and taxis ferrying people to this satellite station. Included in the bustling informal sector is a barber—but not just any ordinary barber. He is depicted by a shabbily handwritten sign saying "MR HAIRCUT" He has a portable shade cloth tent and a poorly laminated page of some possible hairstyles, and there is barely enough space on the sidewalk for pedestrians to avoid stepping onto Hendrick-Verwoerd Highway—a major Johannesburg arterial road.

His name is Teddy and he informs me that it will be R10 for a No.3. No frills. No comfortable chair, no massaged scalp, no beautiful women meticulously manicured. No air con, no music and certainly no privacy. But for one fifth of the usual price what can you expect?

Time is of no real importance, another difference between the old and the new way of life at Big Ben, and although Teddy assures me that he will be finished in "two minutes—chop-chop" he takes considerably shorter than that. After only one glance in the cracked piece of mirror I realise that it is embarrassingly obvious that Teddy has never cut a white man's hair before, nothing resembling a long, straight, thin piece of hair has ever passed through his electric clippers.

There are strands of thatch all over the place as if you'd thrown a chlorine bomb onto an old beach hut.

I take control. White South African males are good at that, and I proceed to empower Teddy to give my head a thorough shaving which he does with the care and concentration of someone brand new to an unfamiliar task.

As I sit on this upturned beer crate and survey the reactions of the passing traffic, I can only begin to laugh. People cocooned in the safety of their locked, alarmed and satellite tracked vehicles, white-knuckled anxiety and fearful anticipation of becoming yet another hijack statistic, are forced to take a second look at the scene on the side of the road.

Smiles start to appear, positive hand signals are gestured, and occasionally, an electric window winds down and something humorous is shouted across the dual carriageway.

Spontaneity. Even in Johannesburg, we are capable of this most precious form of freedom and expression. We have only an instant to jump on the opportunity, and if we miss it, we miss all the magic that it causes, but if seized, the act produces some special outcomes, where, for a moment, barriers are crossed, where we can laugh with each other and at ourselves instead of with ourselves and at each other.

We so often rue the times we weren't spontaneous, and retrospect and hindsight never bring those missed moments back.

To remove the mental barriers, we have is not achieved by Governmental Policy, it occurs gradually as each individual removes one brick at a time. It requires us to alight from our armoured cars, settle on a beer crate and see life from the other side.

I walked away R10 and a heap of hair lighter but with a sense of freedom and an experience that no previous haircut, no matter how posh, has ever offered me.

Here's to you, Teddy, and if you have another straight-haired client, shave up against the grain and tell them to watch the traffic!

P.S. If I could have a haircut right now, I'd teleport myself to visit Bash. Bash works and lives in Downtown Durban, and amongst many other pursuits, he owns and operates a hair salon next to the Denis Hurley Church in Victoria Junction, across the road from Warwick Triangle.

Bash was a professional footballer from Ghana whose career was cut short through injury, and he can talk with authority on most subjects from sport to religion.

He can talk about hardship, but he lives with hope.

One always gets so much more than a haircut from this quality Human Being.

The Still Point in a Turbulent World

The scene could be from a movie. A war movie if you're watching it or a horror movie if you're an extra on the set. In a matter of seconds, half a struggling city's residents are rendered homeless as a few thousand tonnes of Ammonium Nitrate form a lethal combination with a fire and a warehouse of fireworks, and Beirut lies obliterated. Again.

I remember seeing such scenes of devastation in the limited media of the mid-nineteen seventies as a child, and thinking how life could be any worse. A civil war, child soldiers, invasions and political manipulations all built powerful and emotive images in my mind which struggled to find any comprehensible reason for it all.

Nearly half a century later, I watch in awe as the searing white shock wave from the explosion hit my emotional solar plexus harder than the sucker punch I received many years ago from a much larger boy. That had me doubled up in my own pathetic version of 'I can't breathe'!

I deserved that right hook to the body. Nobody—especially the Lebanese people, who have endured millenniums of mismanagement and aeons of upheaval—deserved this. Fifteen years of a civil war were made to look like a left arm throw (for a right hander) in just a few explosive seconds.

With the sound of broken glass been swept up all around her, a 79-year-old grandmother sits at one of the few surviving pieces of furniture in her apartment. The piano is over sixty years old according to her Granddaughter, May Abboud Melki, and like her grandmother, it has survived many things—including a civil war and an equally long Syrian occupation. The window frames of her once tidy apartment lie over the torn lavender coloured upholstery of her sitting room, and the curtain rods resemble a game of giant pick up sticks. Family photos smile defiantly out of their glassless frames in memory of a happier time, and the pot plants on her now open balcony are being restored to their upright position.

While she plays, she wears her mask, and the first two chords are instantly recognisable even to a musical philistine like myself.

The tune is 'Auld Lang Syne', and its playing is as poignant as its meaning. Perhaps she was longing for the sake of, and return to, the old times, and she would have remembered well the paradise and playground of Beirut in the swinging sixties. Could the Scottish poet Robert Burns ever have envisioned that his 1788 penning of this Scottish folk song would be played in the still moment of such devasting destruction? A song about reunions and relationships sung in the humour of Hogmanay, now an air of hope and Humanity in the horror of Lebanon.

Just like the band played on whilst the Titanic sank, this lone pianist teaches us that resilience can be found in the most unlikely of places, and like the Callery Pear tree which survived the 9/11 attacks on New York's twin towers in 2001, she sends out the seedlings of hope.

Every year the seeds of this remarkable 'Survivor Tree' are given to three communities which have endured tragedy in recent years (Wikipedia).

At this challenging time for the world, how on earth do you pick only three?

If hope and resilience were finite concepts, it wouldn't be possible to make this 'Sophie's choice'. Yet these qualities are not finite. They are infinite in that they can't be measured in a linear fashion, and a little hope with a dash of resilience goes a long way.

Just ask a grandmother at her piano playing a timeless piece as she finds that still point in a turbulent world.

And by God, Robert Burns, the world could do with that 'cup o' kindness' you wrote about in days gone by.

BE KIND

In bright colours and written at an ascending angle stands a block letter artwork.

Perhaps it is less of an artwork, and more of a suggestion for Humanity.

It reads 'BE KIND' and it is displayed boldly on the corner of Oxford and Glenhove outside the Standard Bank building and opposite the iconic golden arches of McDonalds. To my great delight, there is another one standing loudly and proudly outside the Constitution Court against the ramparts of the old fort on the dividing line between Hillbrow and Braamfontein, and its message could not be simpler yet more powerful.

We take time with our leadership groups under the trees there, just next to the flame of democracy, and it provides in two simple words, both a platform for reflection and the springboard for debate and action. Without getting into all the unkindness this place has seen in its history, the constitutional court stands here as a beacon of hope for a different future, and perhaps the kindest thing it represents now is how it has masterfully challenged the unkind laws of the past, and upheld the new kindness espoused in our human rights.

A short while ago a good friend of mine launched an initiative for the homeless called *Love is a verb*. Beautiful heart stickers are bought for some pocket change and given to the homeless who in turn are able to sell them to passing motorists as an act of dignified trade rather than one of a desperate begging.

If love is a verb—a doing word which requires action, then surely so too is kindness?

There were two stories this week which highlighted the simple yet profound impact of small acts of kindness.

In the state of Rhode Island, a pizza delivery man by the name of Ryan Catterson delivers a pizza to the Sheely home in West Warwick. The ring video doorbell captures a moving image of two-year-old Cohen running out, after the transaction, to give the man a hug. Mom thinks this is cute, which it is, and posts it on her Instagram page. Ryan gets wind of it and his story unfolds.

While smiling on the outside he has been grieving the unexpected loss of his own daughter Alyssa in the same week, and he speaks of the healing properties of an unsolicited and unscripted hug. He speaks of God, of the universe, and the connection he had with a two-year-old as a moment of truth with his daughter. And in that moment, he finds some peace in his own internal world of turmoil.

Every student has wanted to hug a pizza delivery man at some point in their lives as a promise to the end of a hungover hunger, but I wonder how many ever do? I never have, though I have thought about it often, and it serves as a reminder that kindness, like love, lies in the action, and not just in the thought.

Small spontaneous act. Massive unimagined repercussions.

A second story emerged from the world of sports. Not just any sport—the biggest global sport of football. Not just any league—the most popular league worldwide. At the top of the British premier league is Liverpool, and the man at the helm is Jurgen Klopp. This household name and his club are riding the wave of unprecedented success. The pressure is intense and the demands on his time must be overwhelming.

Jurgen Klopp receives a letter from ten-year-old Daragh Curley who is a passionate Manchester United fan. He asks Klopp to please make sure that Liverpool start losing some games, because this continuous winning streak of his club's bitter rival is making him sad.

Despite the media pressures, the millions of global fans expectations, the training schedules, the travel, the required match focus points and a rare moment for his personal life, Klopp takes time to respond in a privately crafted and personal letter to young Daragh.

In a page of pure genius, and one which should be made compulsory reading for all managers and sports fans alike, he talks of sportsmanship, of responsibility and of respect.

Underpinning all of it lies an act of kindness.

I wonder how many thoughts of kindness have never manifested as acts? How many times I have failed to write the letter of thanks, to stop to help change the tyre, to hold someone's hand across a busy road, to buy the stickers for the homeless, or even greet the security guard at my next corporate meeting?

Whilst a personal letter from the worlds most recognised manager may not sway the allegiance of a dyed in the wool United fan, a hug from a two-year-old may change someone's life.

BE KIND.

The least we can do might mean the most to someone else?

POLARITY 4

IS THE WORLD SEPARATE AND DISCONNECTED, OR IS IT INFINITELY CONNECTED?

The higher goal in this chapter is to embrace integration.

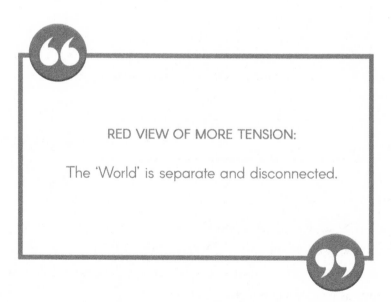

RED VIEW OF MORE TENSION:

The 'World' is separate and disconnected.

Perhaps this view stemmed from the old adage of divide and conquer. We have been comfortable creating pigeon holes and boxes to define people, their actions and even their consumer behaviours. If you are not of the same feather, let's make sure you don't flock together. Keep divisions deep as they are easier to control and support the secrets in the silos. What happens to you is of little concern to me, and as long as the hole is at the other end of the boat, we should remain unaffected. Keep the walls of 'The Stop Nonsense'* strong and its fences well wired, and don't bring your troubles here. Good fences make great neighbours and while it is wise to have some security measures in place, if you lived in the Old South Africa as I did, you will remember this as a devastating system of control called Apartheid.

Thankfully this changed and opened the way to the possibility inherent in a far more connected world.

BLUE VIEW TOWARDS CONNECTION:

'The World' is infinitely connected.

When I 'SEE' a connected world, I can reach out to others of every conceivable walk of life as my 'DO', and the 'GET' is integration. It is far easier to connect the dots and solve the challenges we face if we see ourselves as part of a connected world.

As we journey through the 'Double-up'* into this section, we will meet all sorts of souls who have found connection in their lives. A youth group from KZN, SA who have found a connection to their community through the discipline of savings and homeless, not hopeless, Sifiso who is connected to his work, no matter how humble that work may be. We will hear the sounds of an African choir who have found connection through love, fellowship, and song, and be served by Theodora, a smiling waitress who is connected to her customers.

We will go gardening with Jan Coenraad who is deeply connected to nature and his God. We will meet Patrick, who connected with his purpose and connects still through the presence of the dignified shadow of his significance. We will also swim together in a tidal pool to experience the life-giving flows of fresh waves of connection.

Lastly, we will meet a lone spotted hyena whose life hangs in the balance because he has lost connection with his community.

When we connect, we can begin to belong, and there is not much more important to our overall health and wellbeing than to experience a sense of belonging.

"In a real sense all life is inter-related. All men are caught in an inescapable network of mutuality, tied in a single garment of destiny. Whatever affects one directly, affects all indirectly."

Martin Luther King Jr.

- A 'stop-nonsense' is a wall or fence erected between neighbours in many of the old townships of South Africa. It was not originally designed as an impenetrable barrier to entrance, but merely as a reminder to everyone not to bring 'nonsense' or mischief, or unwanted behaviour into one's space.
- The 'Double-up' is the gate in the fence which most often in those days remained unlocked. The invitation was simple. Come in through the gate.

Apart from making good sense in the connection of community, this system of boundaries and short cuts made it impossible for the South African Police Force (Yes, in the 1960s, it was the police force, not the police service) to control the flow of alcohol, deemed as illegal for people of colour up until 1961.

But that is a subject of another story. With a cold, and legal beer in hand!

A Dog Won't Bite If It's Busy Chewing

"Inja ayilumi uma isahlafuna"

There are two containers situated on a piece of land in a place called Besters in the sprawling urban and peri-urban surrounds of Kwa Mashu in Kwa Zulu Natal, South Africa. On reflection, there are countless more in these areas which double as workshops, cell phone outlets, hair and beauty salon, storage facilities and roadside tuck shops, but these two seem to stand out from the others. They are painted blue, and they have a recently planted and healthily growing vegetable garden on the slope going down towards the road.

For many years up to sixty women and one man met here on Saturday afternoons. They still gather here, but there are a few more men, and there is a youth group now. The physical space has not changed too much for some time, but the possibilities which have emerged from these containers are so radically different to what they once were. There is still the sanguine singing which reverberates out of the tin tympani and across the Zululand valleys, but there is a bit more baritone and bass to the song and to the prayer.

They are here to save money.

Little by little their single South African Rands turn to boxes of washing powder and multiple birthday blankets. Educations have been paid for and houses have been renovated or even built, and if the name of their savings scheme 'Lethu kuhle' is anything to go by, then good things are indeed coming. Not just the men who are more often seen in the taverns, and the youth, but also the ideas, the support and the hope. Perhaps those three things—ideas, support and hope might be enough to build a community. For that is what greets here, meets here and eats here.

As we cram into the already packed containers to learn from their leadership, a young man with the fire of hope in his eyes calls out in an excited voice:

"Inja ayilumi uma isahlafuna".

Had this been in 1879, and a couple of hundred miles North and inland, I might have thought I was about to receive a disembowelling at the hands of King Cetshwayo's victorious Zulu army on the battlefields of Isandlwana. There was both power and passion in his voice, and a response from gogos (Grandmothers) and grandkids alike that they were in agreement and were ready to follow him into battle.

And they are in a battle. An economic battle for survival where they have learned that their only weapon is themselves. Themselves and each other. Battles turn to wars, and wars demand war cries, and a call to arms. They are arming themselves no longer with political power, but with money and knowledge.

"A dog won't bite if it's busy chewing."

This rallying cry rocked me in its raw rurality.

The Fourteenth Century Father of English literature and writer of Olde English classics, Geoffrey Chaucer, had something to say about this in that "idle hands are the Devil's tools", and he probably interpreted this from the Bible's Book of Proverbs 16:27, and the Turks have a wisdom that everyone is tempted by the Devil, but idle people tempt the Devil.

The Zulu version cut me to the core in the word 'bite'.

When I am busy in my own life, I don't have time to bite. I have no interest to harm others when I engage in my own meaningful work. I don't bite into the meaningless universe of remote-controlled channels of repeated reruns (unless the golf is on), and I don't bite at my children out of boredom. When I am busy chewing, I don't sit too long tippling at the tavern of travail and temptation or banging on the bar of boredom and blame. I get off the couch of slouch and I go for a stroll in the suburbs or a swim in the golden light off the sea. When I am detached, I look for inspiration in a device, but when I am engaged, my inspiration is right across the table in the unasked light of my children's own chewings.

What was the best thing that happened today? And the worst? And if I stop long enough to listen to the stories of the tennis or cricket, or water polo or dream dress, I stop biting at the blank spaces of an uncertain future, and I fill the present with presence. I enjoy the conversation even more than the meal, and I don't rush off to the same looped CNN latest update.

I phone a friend in the traffic on the way home instead of biting at the next taxi driver, and I turn off the TV to read something far more meaningful.

When I am bored, I bite. The bite does not always show up as a violent temper tantrum, it could be far more painful and poisonous in dismissive disengagement or snide cynicism. What could be more damaging to a child's view of the world than the negative reflection of someone they look to for guidance?

When our global level of employee engagement is dismally low and trending downwards, and the unemployment of our youth in South Africa hovers on the wrong side of half, something will bite. And it may bite at the coffee stations and water coolers in the passages of perceived politically correct politeness, or it may bite in the next rock thrown in a protest against poor service delivery. While it may look like life-giving water from afar, the acid of anger will eat us from the inside, unless we have something else to get stuck into and occupy our minds.

Interesting phrase that, "get stuck in." Perhaps it is the quickest way of becoming unstuck?

While the Youth at Besters are here to save money, as they do so, they also find meaning and purpose. They share stories of fear and excitement, of despair and hope. They have a community to eat with and there's less time and reason to bite.

They save themselves in this way, and nothing is more dangerous than the venom of our own vindictiveness towards ourselves.

The Real Wealth of Work

Anyone from the area known as The Parks in Johannesburg will know of Delta Park. In the 'Big Smoke', this is a restful and respiratory green lung of over a hundred hectares and it provides a welcome playground for many of the city's residents. If you know Delta Park, then you will know the Blue Bridge—an iconic landmark allowing passage over the Braamfontein Spruit, and a meeting point for pelotons of peddlers, rafts of runners, wanderings of walkers and of course a defecation of dogs. Whilst these are not the official collective nouns of these groupings, perhaps they paint a more vivid picture.

Especially the defecation of dogs.

Hundreds, if not thousands of dogs can be seen in the Delta over a weekend, and most leave a calling card which is their own Facebook posting and attracts a faecal fascination of man's best friends. Whilst there is a Johannesburg law against this form of canine clutter, like most laws in this extraordinary place, a blind eye becomes a pair, and even a nasal passage is conveniently, and suddenly blocked to any offensive evidence.

Since lock down has eased, there has been an increase in traffic of all types, and the car guards along Marlborough are well and truly back in business. On my last few visits there, I have also met up with Sifiso who is most often encountered at the Blue Bridge. Armed with a poop scoop and a green plastic bag, he wears his pink size five hand me down cross trainers with pride, even though he is a size seven. He is reading *The Book Thief* by Markus Zusak, which takes up a great deal of space in his backpack and it is immediately clear that the book is not just there for show when he gently takes my notebook and pen in his gloved hands to write down a phrase in isiZulu.

He takes great pains and patience to describe each word, and I know that the stubborn secretary of my linguistic left brain will probably never file the sentence correctly for a fluent recall from the far reaches of the banks of my memory. What I won't forget though, is the meaning behind this phrase which this homeless philosopher helped me to truly grasp.

"When a child is born its hands are closed to show the world it is holding a gift; when a person dies, their hands are open to show that they have let go of this world."

Sifiso Sithole lost his job as an office administrator and his children live with their mother, and yet, he walks these pathways and cleans up the debris left by the dogs of The Delta. As he greets some of the regulars, he smiles in the realisation that one dogs turds are another man's treasure, and he says that although he would prefer not to do this forever, he will do what he can right now. He saw a need, showed up to serve, and he is able to send some money to his young daughter.

Mahatma Gandhi 'the great one' wrote about work, and this extract is portrayed in Number Four jail at Constitution Hill where he was imprisoned a number of times in the early 1900's:

"It is wrong to think of any work as humiliating or degrading. I saw that sometimes there was an argument about who should carry the bucket for urine. If we had understood the full meaning of Satyagraha, [holding onto truth] we would have competed with one another in doing such work." MK Gandhi

I left with so much more than an immaculately written phrase in my notebook. I left with an overwhelming gratitude for the work I still have. That as much as this Covid-19 virus has decimated my job, I still have work, and I only hope I can give to that work, the same open-handed attitude with which Sifiso gives to his serving. Could I arrive with my gifts held tight, leave them all on the table of my life in total surrender, just to depart this world showing a pair of open hands with nothing left to give?

In these times when rightfully, so many are demanding to be seen, I wonder if who I'm being is worthy of being seen, and whether the work I do is worth giving with an open hand?

I guess I have a better chance of being seen if I am truly grateful for the work I do, and if that work carries worthy purpose. Work is perhaps so much more than a means to accumulate wealth. It is what gets us up physically, moves us emotionally and serves us spiritually, and it matters not whether we are corporate directors or collectors of dung.

Like so many things in life, we moan about it when it's around, but we miss it when it's gone and maybe the real wealth of work lies not in <u>what</u> we do, but rather in <u>how and why</u> we do that work.

Sawubona Sifiso. I see you. Your work and your life matter greatly.

Steve Hall

"Uma Ingani izalwa izandla zivalekile ukubonisa upethe izipho zalomhlaba.

Uma umuntu ashona izandlwa ziyavuleka ukubonisa ukuthi uyazidedela ezomhlaba."

With thanks to Sifiso Sithole. Philosopher.

The Choir

The wedding ceremony was almost complete. As the emotional yet beaming bride emerged from the registry with her new lifelong partner, the choir burst into a traditional isiZulu wedding march and blessing. There were broad smiles, teary eyes, tapping feet, and even a little jig from the happy couple, the mother of the bride, and the father of the groom— such was the irresistible powerful charm of the Union Bible Institute Choir.

While best wishes were wished and confetti snowed down over the newly-weds, the choir faded out quietly through the back and enjoyed some refreshments ready for the trip home. There was an unmistakable buzz after their singing that seemed at a higher level than the anticipatory excitement that usually precedes the reception and it was an opportunity on which to capitalise and capitalise quickly. The singers piled into the waiting minibuses, and being one of the fortunate drivers, I asked if they would sing as we drove past the congregation who were milling around outside the beautiful Hilton College chapel.

What a question! It needed no repetition, no subsequent reasoning or justification, and certainly no begging or bribery. And what a resounding answer. No hesitation, no embarrassment, no shyness, and no musical accompaniment. Only their God-given voices, their enthusiasm and their overwhelming desire to abundantly share what they loved.

We left the smiling and waving wedding guests, ambled slowly and jubilantly into the enveloping Midlands mist, and drove down through the spectacular grounds to the gate. I thought their voices would start to fade out quietly considering we were now out of sight and certainly out of earshot from the crowd. I was mistaken, gloriously mistaken.

They did not stop.

With every passing face along the road, they sang louder. As I tapped my hands on the steering wheel and danced in the seat of my car they sang more freely, and when wafts of mist closed in around us, I was only too pleased to be forced to slow down and stretch the moment. The goose bumps on my neck were visible in the rear-view mirror and the image reflected back was almost shockingly happy. I could not remove the smile I had and my worries were simply melting in the mist. I eased off even further on the accelerator—if there was traffic behind me, it would simply have to wait. I had no conscience and was unconscious of time. Each new song was like a thirteenth cheque, and the thought of money cropped up.

I have a six shuttle CD player, amplifier, and up to two hundred watts of music system installed in my combi, and they remained silently in shame. The power in their voices, and the complete absence of distortion made advanced technology sound totally redundant. It was a moment of supreme spirituality—a short fifteen-kilometre journey which took me to my own Heaven and back.

How many moments like this were missed a few years ago? We might never know. But the opportunity we now have to discover more of them is astounding. With people like these——true messengers of God who spread a way of life just by living it, there is hope, and plenty of it. They take their problems, and there are plenty of them in an area of unrest, with an upright posture and straight on the chin and they give back only love and fellowship. Love and fellowship and song.

I imagine that with these three attributes alone we could address so many of the problems we still have as a nation.

We eventually arrived back at their church and I reluctantly switched off the car. We bowed our heads together in spontaneous prayer, and although I had no idea of the meaning of the words, the message was overwhelmingly simple.

Love, fellowship and song.

God bless us all and God bless Africa, and above all, God bless you the Union Bible Institute, all those like you and all the lives you touch.

P.S It is not long now until my own wedding. An African choir will be present.

P.P.S The message was simple once more. Love, fellowship, and song.

"I Live in This World"

'Thank You for your poem.'

I looked up from my Monday morning diary to see the familiar smiling face of Theodora. Her gleaming white teeth sparkled against the blemish and wrinkle free ebony of her perfect African skin which is so often the envy of regular salon goers who would part with good money and endure expensive and painful procedures to achieve such a result.

I knew exactly which poem she was referring to, but I was struggling to connect the dots of how she had received the piece.

It had been no more than forty-two hours since the Springboks had dished out a rugby lesson to the confident English team in the final of the Rugby World Cup in Japan in 2019, and most of that forty-two hours since then had been a blur for the majority of South Africans who had celebrated a sensational victory. I had written a poem during the game in an effort to keep my own emotions in check as I have a penchant (a

French word in light of there being a French referee) for losing my cool and shouting at said referee through a TV screen in the belief that they will change their decisions from a loud enough armchair criticism. The poem was read out to a smattering of young boys, and a few dads at the final whistle. A close friend had recorded it, sent it out to a few mates, and—the rest, as they say —went viral.

Within hours, I had received messages from people still in the stadium in Tokyo, a family in Dubai, a friend in Canada, my rugby playing nephew in the UK whose smile at the victory was impossibly larger than usual as he was surrounded by his Richmond Rugby Club mates. The comments poured in from a host of other interesting and far-off places.

All these connections were running through a dulled and discombobulated mind as I looked up at the smiling Theodora who in her customary way was still holding my Americano in her right hand, and holding her right hand gently in her left. I have come to learn that this is a symbolic act in both the giving and receiving of gifts or blessings. One gives and receives with both hands for then one is truly grateful or appreciative. It is as if one is giving fully of themselves, and being fully present in the moment of ceremony. One hand is not stuck in a pocket or attached to a cell phone. Both are given to the relationship—anything else might be considered rude.

As I accepted (with both hands) the steaming cup of caffeine, a medicinal miracle on such a Monday morning, she could no doubt read my confusion as I stammered through a condescending sounding response:

"Theodora, how did you get the poem."

Perhaps I had put more emphasis on the word 'you' than would show up in black and white type, but her response was as gentle as her smile and as swift as her service:

"I live in this world."

Not for the first time—and probably not the last, either—my perception of myself as a transformed and evolved white South African male had been shattered.

"I live in this world."

Why, for one moment had I thought she didn't? Why did I assume she didn't have access to social media? Or that she probably never watched the rugby? Or that she was in some way incapable of joining the dots far quicker than I could have in that moment?

Perhaps I learned right there, that the blinkers we have on the way we see the world need constant removal, the lenses of our viewpoints require regular maintenance, and although our eyes remain the same colour for most of our lives, the colour they see and the assumptions which follow may need ongoing cleansing for clarity.

Had I really based my thoughts, and dare I say judgements on the colour of her skin, her gender or the job she was doing serving me coffee in the coffee shop of my son's school as I strategically avoided the Johannesburg morning traffic?

I have paid a lot more attention to Theodora since then—if even in a more welcoming and thankful smile as she hurries about like a nurse tending to the early morning demands of a largely post weekend deflated clientele.

Theodora comes from Venda near a place called Thoyandou in the Province of Limpopo. She has four of her own children, and another five which she has adopted from both a Brother and a Sister who have passed on.

Nine children. One job.

Oscar Wilde, an Irish play write and poet once said:

"To live is the rarest thing in the world, most people just exist."

Theodora would do well to just exist on a small income and a broad set of responsibilities, yet she does more than this. She lives fully as she smiles and serves… and offers her thanks to unsuspecting people for their poetry.

You do live in this world Theodora, and because of you many others do too.

I can only imagine those nine smiling faces welcoming you back on your next trip home.

I will see you next Monday with clearer eyes and a smile… And both hands will be out graciously as I accept a coffee poured with love.

P.S. Here is the poem I wrote during that epic final. That game may have only been eighty minutes of linear time between the first and the last blast of the referee's whistle, but it stopped the clock of a nation, and we will no doubt relive the euphoria many times over.

It was for all South Africans an unforgettable Kairos moment.

SIYABONGA SPRINGBOKS

It's been twelve long years and that's a long wait

And for most of those years we've been in a bad state

A state of corruption and dark nights without power

And short splashes of water when taking a shower.

But despite all this, the energy's been rising

Maybe, just maybe, there'd be something surprising

A World Cup final to roll back the years

And images of Madiba which still bring us to tears.

From Peterhouse to Grey, social media's alive

As they've urged our Springboks to keep up their drive

Messages from Rassie—Thanks for all your support

This brave rugby team's so much more than just sport.

You see they've shown us as a country, how to Unite

Their love for each other's a remarkable sight

The Ndlovu choir has sung with elation

With each spirited tweet we could rebuild our nation.

Fifty-Seven million sang from the depths of their hearts

And our fifteen fine men had the purest of starts

With fleet footed attacks and four Pollard kicks

The half time scoreboard read twelve points to six!

Perhaps our whole country was praying to God

And perhaps God was listening, coz' on came the Bomb Squad

Our front row had smashed them in all but one scrum

The English would rather be at home with their Mum!

As the clock ticked down, we carried on praying

And our boys dug deep in their passionate playing

A chip from Mapimpi and Am's moment of magic

And a second Brexit looked ever so tragic!

Then suddenly a moment we were all waiting for

Our X Factor Cheslin unpicked a locked door

The mercurial player seemed to make his own spaces

As he put smiles on the dials of a whole Nations faces.

For twelve years our Rugby glory's been starved

But with three minutes to go, the trophy was carved

We stand by you, Heroes, as you bring home the cup

You've lifted a nation and you've lifted us up.

Eish, Zuma, Sorry, you've not lifted this prize

But you've lifted enough before our own eyes

This country's amazing—it tells a hell of a story

And perhaps now is the time we find our true glory.

From Alex to Zwide we'll dance in the street

The Braai's will burn long as we drink and we eat

You've shown us the art of pure dragon slaying

I don't know about you, but # I'm staying!

You've done us so proud with your hearts full of passion

Can we help you Cyril, bring SA back into fashion?

For so long now we've been at the end of our tether

But one thing's for sure we're # Stronger Together!

Steve Hall

Souls of St Francis

I first arrived in St Francis as a thirteen-year-old boy in August of 1983. The canals were small and the beach was wide; the old hotel with its Cutty Sark Bar and off-sales was the 'Legends' of the time. Before rumours fester into facts, I only went there because they had a pool table, and it was a place to play when the weather on the 'Maxwell 9' was at its most unfriendly.

It did not take long to fall in love with this bay; even my father—who was vehemently against owning a second home—was sold. Just two holidays later, he walked into a possible rental and declared no intention to rent. He wanted to buy.

And so, we became the proud owners of Nautilus and—somewhat surprisingly, a 1970-something Isuzu diesel bakkie, which became affectionately known as 'The Goat Boat'. It used to have the high railings typical of a livestock transporter, and when packed with teenagers, it prompted my mother to comment that we all looked like a bunch of goats. The name had stuck ever since, and though the railings have long since rusted away along with most of her under carriage, the engine has never failed.

Not once.

It has never failed either to draw a smile from passers-by, and remains the preferred mode of transport today for my own teenagers.

My father has always loved gardens. He would far rather be digging with a spade than hacking divots off the fairways, and planting seedlings over planting himself on the beach. In the December of 1986—our first Christmas holiday in our new home—he spent the full four weeks carving a path to the sea through the Rhus and the Port Jackson.

He needed help, and he found it in another soul of St Francis by the name of Jan Coenraad. Jan was equally fond of gardens, and as a result of their efforts, the community garden today stands proudly from halfway up Harbour road down to Granny's Pool and forms the first few hundred metres of the Port-to-Port walk. Over the years, there have been weddings and memorial services here, joined by countless bird watchers, picnickers, photographic shoots, treasure hunts, Easter egg explorations, and more than a few holiday romance rendezvous away from the prying eyes of parents.

Jan was a man of God, and a man of the Earth. One day, when taking a break for his customary cup of tea and a sandwich on his son Pieter's memorial bench, he was approached by an old friend of the family.

"Sjoe, Jan, Mr Hall keeps you busy here."

Jan looked up towards Port Elizabeth. He stared through the wrinkles of his well weathered eye sockets and winked up at the heavens through his sparkling eyes, and in the dry and respectful humour he was loved for replied:

"Ja, dankie Here vir die see." (Yes, thank you, God, for the sea.)

It was his observation that if it wasn't for the sea, there would be no end to his work.

Jan would no doubt, if he was still alive today, be proud of the Port-to-Port walk —even if that meant to Port Elizabeth.

Yes, St Francis has many ways to please one's heart; but it is really the souls of this place which capture it and hold it whether they are still alive or not.

For souls live on regardless. You need only to walk through Jan's garden to know that.

A Heart Which Still Beats

Patrick Magebhula Hunsley, founding member and stalwart of the South African Alliance and Shack Dwellers International (SDI) died on the 4th August 2014.

Since the early 1990s, Patrick was instrumental in building community networks and local savings schemes. He negotiated with Government departments, and even turned away offers when it jeopardised the needs of the community. From his home in Piesang River between the shack lands of Inanda, Durban, where the Federation built 1,431 houses between 1992 and 2000, Patrick mobilised communities across South Africa as a leader of the Federation of the Urban and Rural Poor.

Since 2008/09 he served as the chairperson of the Informal Settlement Network. He built progressive partnerships with Government agencies and as a special adviser to the previous minister of human Settlements Mr. Tokyo Sexwale, served as a committee member of the Ministerial Sanitation Task Team, and presented at numerous international conferences such as World Urban Forum 7.

(Extract from 'Know Your City' Website)

We would visit Patrick on Sundays. His welcome was even warmer than his wide smile. Patrick was—and still is, even long after his passing—a catalyst for conversation, a model of mobilisation and the embodiment of empowerment. We would learn lessons from him not only about savings, but also about salvation; not only about housing, but also about Humanity.

He was the inspiration behind many hundreds of savings groups in KwaZulu Natal, and nationally. Those meetings would start with an impassioned rallying cry, a call to action; "Amandla!"

And the response:

"Imali Nolwaz!"

Roughly translated, "Power comes through money and knowledge."

The money side seemed obvious. Get together and save—we are #stronger together. And incredibly, from these humble beginnings, people have been able to build their own houses, bigger, better, and cheaper than a standard RDP house.

Power through knowledge however, was perhaps even more important. As these groups would gather, they would learn about each other. They would really know their neighbour, and this more than anything would build their community.

While Patrick may have initiated some of these ideas, in true Patrick style, he always handed them over to someone else—and always to a woman. He would always explain three reasons why:

1) They are far better with money, and will put it to the advancement of their community before their personal consumption (and here he would take an imaginary swig of beer).

2) They are connected, they talk, and they know exactly why someone wasn't at the meeting and could see through excuses as to where that five Rand went yesterday.

3) They are more approachable.

There are three great lessons of leadership right there.

Patrick's isiThunzi, his Seriti—his dignified shadow of significance—lives on, and painted on the inside wall of his office in Piesang River near Inanda, is the following inscription:

"Our lives are very short so we cannot afford to close them to others… We need to open the doors to our hearts, minds and communities, by doing this we will learn from each other, they will learn from our heart failures, we will live through their heartbeats, how will they know if we don't let them in?"

Whilst his lungs may have stopped breathing, his heart still beats strongly.

Patrick 'let us in' and we are still so much the richer for his presence and the warm shadow of his significance.

Teachings of a Tidal Pool

I am fairly sure that my earliest memories of the Seaside were on the South coast of KwaZulu Natal between Scottburgh and Clansthal.

The Blue Marlin Hotel was the iconic family getaway with a kids' dining room as a main attraction. It was not so much for the children's entertainment, but rather for some adult sanity. As a parent myself now, I have fond memories of enjoying an uninterrupted bottle of wine while the mayhem of a miniature meal is consumed in a separate environment of controlled chaos.

I learned to hold my breath underwater in this haven for holiday makers. On Saturdays, the hotel entertainment staff would unload a few cases of canned beverages into the swimming pool. The children were allowed one dive each to gather what we could, and then bask in the sun with our liquid loot.

I learned that if the labels on the tins read Lion Lager or Castle Lager, they would fetch a much higher price with the adults on the sun loungers around the pool willing to pay a long and lazy dollar for an afternoon aperitif. The monies earned from a good dive could last well into the week with cold bottles of Cokes and Fanta orange from the local tuck shop. I am still convinced that no Coca Cola has ever tasted better than it did out of a thick glass bottle in the early nineteen-seventies.

For most of the rest of my days there, I remember spending hours exploring the rock and tidal pools.

Many decades later, these beautiful coastal features still hold an extraordinary fascination, and not unsurprisingly, I have found myself in an equally engaging relationship with some unique characters in a gathering fittingly called the Tidal Pool.

In a recent online meeting, one of our calm and colourful inhabitants held us all spellbound with an obvious, yet refreshingly new analogy of who we might be as a gathering called the Tidal Pool. With deep gratitude to Sarah Campbell-Watts for the beauty of the analogy and some humble apologies if I spin the thinking out of the intertidal zone boundaries of reason.

It is an analogy which really caused me to hold my breath. This time not to dive for adult beverages, but to delve deep for a different treasure in reflection, relation, and resonance.

On my first opportunity to walk along the coastline since lock down, I wandered down to the rocks to think more deeply and to contemplate the gift of this intriguing idea.

I watched as wave after wave rolled in, and observed that while tidal pools offer some comfort and protection from the harshness of a wild open ocean, that guard is never guaranteed. High tides arrive and low tides leave, and each one brings or takes something with them. Fresh, nutrient-enriched water splashes in along with a range of new possibilities and interesting and unique pool partners. Change happens with every new wave and is embraced quickly as coastal chaos is restored to a new order.

I stopped for a moment to stare through a narcissistic reflection, and started to notice the enormous detail and abundant diversity in even the smallest of rock pools. Soft, velvety tentacles of a pastel hued sea anemone lay next to and seemed to lick the sharp spines of darkly coloured sea urchins with the caress of a hundred tongues. Both were made more beautiful by the presence of the other.

Perfectly plump pumpkin shells lay delicately wedged in a whelkome of whelks, and the blend was a mixture of robust rigidity with a finite fragility. A curious yet cautious rock wrasse peered out from under his sheltering rock, a crab sidled sideways for a better grip on the iridescent green weed and away from the cascading waterfall of the last wave of disruption, and the shell home of a shuffling hermit relocated without the need of a permit.

These ecosystems are vibrantly alive in their vitality and in their vulnerability.

In my youth, I might have stayed there all day. But as time has marched on, my ankles are prone to twisting around the uneven ground of an intertidal zone. With the day presenting the perfect opportunity for nine holes of golf at a quite different church, I walked back up to higher ground.

I became aware of less and less life in the tidal pools the further away I walked from the action. The outliers seemed to be stagnant with an oily film on the water's still surface and some old sea foam still decorated the sun-bleached rocks. There was little movement, if any at all, and there was a desperate drabness and an air of despair to the isolated inaction of the higher pools.

I looked back at the energy of the lower pools. That energy didn't seem to be present when there was a lack of connection, the further away I moved from the action.

I played a great nine holes. My mind was clear of the usual mess of swing thoughts, and I focused on three key insights and a range of still developing questions.

1) Could I see the tidal pool of my own family as a place of refuge, but not a place of perennially padded protection? How will my children ever know the magic of the sea if they live always in the

confines of the same certainties of a privileged pool?

2) How will I continue to see that inclusivity adds way more than it can ever take away? I would like to be awash with new ideas and options as I face my own waves of change, and those will only come from a celebratory welcoming of diversity.

3) To stay truly alive, I must remain connected. Like any ecosystem that is shut off in isolation, I will die if I don't receive, and I will die if I don't give back. I may be high up in the hierarchy, but it can be lonely. Besides, the fight for oxygen is more intense with every ambition of altitude.

In the spirit of an open pool, please take any of these thoughts with you.

And of course, I will be greatly enriched by any you might choose to leave behind?

With gratitude to Sarah Campbell-Watts for her wave of wisdom.

P.S. My 'Uncle' Butch—Godfather, Marine Biologist, and Philosopher amongst many other things, has thrown a few more pebbles of profundity into the pool as he so often does, and here is another ripple of realisation which will keep my mind focused on flow and not side-lined by swing thoughts.

4) Rock pools all face times of plenty and times of stress. There is a long-term seasonality to these swings and an everyday rhythm to the tides. They could be plundered by poachers and punished by pollution. Could I practice the same balance of tolerance and resilience in the cycles of my own uncertain life?

5) …

(The ellipsis is there for further contributions. Like a healthy tidal pool, it remains open to new ideas and fresh waves of input. Please add abundantly—our ecosystem will be all the richer for your thought!)

Community

Hyenas are curious creatures, and on a typical bushveld morning, a young one slunk silently and secretively through the camp and peered through the netted gauze of tent 8.

It is not a regular occurrence to see these oft maligned predators, and to see one at such close quarters held both a fear and fascination in the same moment. He turned up later in the staff bathroom, and for their and our safety had to be darted in order to be extracted.

It was clear that this animal had some real challenges. A broken leg — which had quite miraculously healed almost straight, but still carried a large lump of calcified bone—caused a slight dragging of his left hind leg. His lungs coughed intermittently throughout his drugged slumber because of an infection, and there were bite marks everywhere; the most obvious of which were around the head and the face, but many more were hidden under the coarse and matted hair.

All of this we learned through the tutorage of the local vet, Mike Toft, whose leadership was as astounding as his gentle care. As he pushed and prodded, pumped and patched, one got the sense that he was also praying for the wellbeing of this injured scavenger. Syringes full of pink and white cocktails were injected into the canine caused cavities, and the flushing antibiotics and antiseptics would emerge from another part of the poor victim's body.

Mike, who would look as at home as a teacher in a school room as he was beside an operating table, was not going to give him great odds. Probably fifty-fifty, which is mouth-watering if you're entering a lotto, but less palatable when the wrong side of the coin is tickets and not just tails, or hopefully Heaven and not only heads.

On many occasions, this kind-natured surgeon may have let nature take its course; but this fighter deserved a chance, and besides, he was yet to face his biggest challenge.

You see, he had lost his community.

How critical is that in my own life? Who am I without one? Would my chances even be as good as the spin of a coin from the fickle finger of fate if I did not belong?

With apologies to Descartes, in Africa I belong therefore I am, and if I belong, I will survive. I will still drag my foot as I walk, or bleed from the head or feel a break in my heart. I may still feel scared or lost or lonely at times, but my community gives me purpose and it gives me protection.

It is my responsibility to give to that community to whom I am connected. To care for it and to cultivate it.

The reward is life. Life worth living fully.

P.S. The last few days, a newly-imposed stage 4 of lockdown has allowed us to take to the streets for a few hours in the early morning.

On day one of this privilege, I walked the roads of our neighbourhood, and covered the princely sum of around four hundred metres.

It took me over an hour.

The rest of the time, I talked and listened—probably in that order— and I realised once more the true value of community. To see people face-to-face. To watch their children on bikes and in prams. To see old friends and new neighbours greet each other, and to re-establish a sense of connection.

For me, these were the real privileges.

Perhaps this will be one of the great opportunities of this new normal, where in the true sense of the Zulu meaning of 'Neighbour', we can rebuild.

"Umakhelwana".

The root of the meaning lies in "to build". To build for one another, and then be built for by one another.

Just like a young hyena, we too can be restored to individual physical health, but we always have a better chance when we belong to a community.

POLARITY 5

ARE WE SUPERIOR OR INFERIOR, OR ARE WE UNIQUE?

The higher goal in this section is to move towards collaboration.

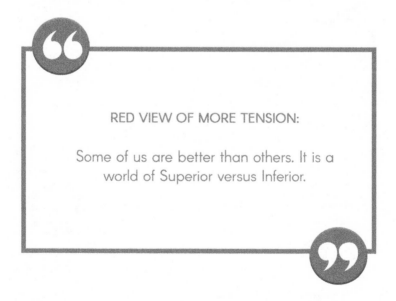

RED VIEW OF MORE TENSION:

Some of us are better than others. It is a world of Superior versus Inferior.

This paradigm of the world around us seems all too painfully prevalent at times. Perhaps it is the birthplace of the potentially evil twins of competition and comparison. I say potentially, because there is a place for competition of course, and maybe we should be comparing ourselves to who we were yesterday so that we can grow into a better version of ourselves tomorrow. However, if competition remains my primary focus, I may end up employing some underhand tactics to support my picture of superiority. Naturally there will be World Cup winners and Olympic Gold medallists, and so there should be. These prizes are just reward for hard work, talent or team dynamics which have been forged together in an agreed upon set of rules for a period of time. So, whilst someone may not be a better runner than the next, it doesn't mean they might not be a better chef, or mother, or birdwatcher. To subscribe only to this point of view is to walk with blinkers on in a narrow and linear, and likely lonely journey.

There is another way which our world is waiting for.

BLUE VIEW TOWARDS CONNECTION:

We are all unique.

To say that the opposite side of this continuum is a view that we are all equal, is also not the full picture. Yes, we may have equal rights—although that too is questionable. A fifteen-year-old teenager has no right to drive a car in South Africa, and neither is she allowed to drink alcohol or vote. Equal opportunities and equal responsibilities are both noble pursuits, but the real magic of the opposite side of this polarity is that we are all unique. Not one of the around 8 Billion human beings is the same. We have different talents, networks, experiences, circumstances and ways of seeing the world.

Think back to the twenty-six letters of the English alphabet. The twelve musical notes. The three primary colours.

It is because of their uniqueness that we live in a world of literature, are moved by the moods of music, and held spellbound by the spiritual sights of the diverse world around us.

When I 'SEE' uniqueness, my 'DO' is to move closer to others, and the 'GET' is a real shot at collaboration.

There is no need and no use for collaboration if we are all the same. No country ever won a Rugby World Cup with fifteen flyhalves—no matter how mercurial they may have been.

In this stage of the journey, we will be stopped in our tracks by a question from a carwash, and another question which made me think more deeply about my own embarrassing attitude of superiority towards women. We will have a look at the uniqueness which lies in our names, and the stories of meaning which birthed them. We will meet a one-of-a-kind punctuation mark which embraces and blends the diversity of a spontaneous surprise with a curious question. Let's sit together in a smoky bar in Copenhagen, and soak up the uniqueness of jazz music, and meet with William who shows us the value of green shoots through his scarred but shining eyes. We will round off this chapter with an old grandmother and a gecko who embrace their own authenticity, and a thought about one of the most unique things we all have available to us. Our choices.

"To be nobody but yourself in a world which is doing its best day and night to make you like everybody else means to fight the hardest battle which any human being can fight; and never stop fighting"

e. e. cummings

A Carwash kind of Question

A carwash is not a carwash is not a carwash.

Just like leadership comes in multiple shapes and forms, so too do many seemingly menial things like a simple carwash. In the smart and sublime suburbs of Sandton, they may be fully automated with a Seattle coffee thrown in as part of the deal. Housewives may have enough time to apply another layer of lacquer to their impatiently tapping talons, while house-husbands run in to buy milk and bread, and for a catch up on WhatsApp.

Many mobile and manual operators walk the mall corridors in their wellies and talk with their toolkits as they solicit a shine with their smiles or pocket a price with a polish.

At golf clubs, an out of bag caddie may offer you a carwash, and even at traffic lights, there will often be someone who steps out of the shadows with an old rag and a seriously diluted bottle of Sunlight soap to clean a windscreen. The end result of this is usually not so much a cleaner visage, but rather a more thinly spread veneer of city smog or ghetto grease. You can guarantee that as you drive through any of the former townships in South Africa, from Soweto to Sea Vista or Tembisa to Thokoza, you will find as many carwashes as you will find hair salons and cell phone outlets. Connectivity, fashion and clean cars are as common in Kwa Thema as they are in Khayalitsha and whether in Ga-Rankuwa or Gugulethu or from Duncan Village to Diepsloot, there is always an opportunity to pamper yourself or pimp your ride. Appearances matter no matter where you live.

Here in F Section of Kwa Mashu, just North West from Durban, there is a social hub with a liquor outlet and enough shaded seating to savour a shared swig from a big bottle of cold beer, or sip from a 'cell phone'—the original half brick sized, mobile shaped, half jack filled with one's favoured flavour which makes one talk! Naturally there is a beauty parlour offering unnatural hair extensions, a spaza shop selling an eclectic collection of consumables, and around the perimeter, fires are lit in half cut forty-four-gallon steel drums for any desire to self-cater. It seems as though the invitation is simple.

Bring it, or buy it—as long as you braai it. Sit for a while and eat, or take it with you down the street. Not too many rules.

The dress code is equally comfortable. Most shirts are worn unbuttoned if worn at all, and being barefoot is as acceptable as the stepping out of some 'shiny shoes' as a passing wedding party pulls in for cigarettes to settle the senses or to arrange a post wedding date.

Here, children play never ending games with limited resources, and their imagination never needs to be recharged or reignited with a software upgrade. There is hardly a stern word from any adult authority, and supervision is superfluous.

In amongst this, there also happens to be a carwash.

Music of all descriptions tumbles from open trunks and beats from boots. Jazz jumps in from a JBL speaker, Rhythm and Blues meets Reggae, Soul slides in from a Citroën, Rap keeps knocking and there is nothing quiet about Kwaito. Whitney Houston is alive and well as she continues to serenade us all as wannabe bodyguards in her proclamation of "I will always love you."

That was the song playing loudest at the moment the driver of the wedding party winked at a freshly extended young hairstyle adorning a knowing smile. In fact, we were sure his conversation went something like this:

"I have nothing, but I wanna dance with somebody. Give me one moment in time, I will run to you, and show you the greatest love of all."

His entire pick-up line summed up in Whitney's song titles. Whether she picked this up or not, her return wink was convincing. Genius comes in multiple shapes and forms too.

I only hoped that the next morning he wouldn't have to ask the painful post party questions of:

"Didn't we almost have it all, and where do broken hearts go?"

I have digressed. It is what a carwash of this nature does to one.

Extraordinary places attract extraordinary characters, and across the carwash came a question so golden that it matched the gold teeth from which it intimidatingly emanated.

"Hey, who are you?"

From the moment Humanity stepped out of the cave and started to climb the ladder of Maslow's hierarchy of needs towards the apex of self-actualisation, we have been held limited and liberated by this question. Everybody from poets to play writes to priests, philosophers to philanthropists, sages to psychologists, coaches, consultants, hypnotists, healers, and helpers have all asked it in various guises. It has been weaved through the fabric of fellowships, stitches of society, and tapestry of tribes. Who we are cuts through the constricting cloth of culture, the organograms of organisations, the row of race, and the rhetoric of religion.

Many have made a living from asking this question.

Some have made a life by answering it.

The Oracle of Delphi advised: "Know Thyself", and Shakespeare continued some three thousand years later: "This above all: to thine own self be true…"

The Rabbi Abraham Twerski was once complimented for having written over fifty books. His humble response was that perhaps he had only written one book, but in over fifty different ways. The bulk of his work was around self-esteem, and one way he explored this was through a similar sort of question: "Without a job, who are you?"

He quite beautifully describes self-esteem as "the true and accurate awareness of one's skills, capabilities and limitations."

On our Leading with Humanity experiences, we try hard to create a space for people to dig deep to find their roots, and there is a life's work to be done just with Twerski's description. The search of course never ends as we try to define ourselves away from attachments and closer to our cores, but every now and then, a question might remind us that we are always on a journey in a constantly changing context.

What was our response in that moment?

Varied. As different and unique as we all are as individual pilgrims.

But right there, in the cauldron of a Kwa Mashu carwash with its camaraderie and conviviality we heard the challenge and I think we found a little more of what we were looking for.

Who am I?

A golden question if ever there was one.

An Embarrassing Epiphany

I only buy the Sunday Times for one reason. The puzzle page. The combination of the cross fit of crosswords and the mental gymnastics of the Giant Sudoku can keep me occupied for hours, and while the rest of the paper is consigned to the scrap heap within minutes of its opening, Heaven help anyone in the house who even dares to move the hallowed puzzle page.

In amongst these language and mathematical challenges is something called Brain Test, by Trivia Tom. There are always twenty questions, and I feel ever so highly educated when I answer them correctly, and even more clever when I justify my excuses for the wrong answer or when I have no answer at all. I wasn't even born then. Hate Opera at the best of times. Stupid Sport to waste time on knowing, and of course, who the hell knows that rubbish, anyway?

This Sunday, August 9th 2020, and fittingly Woman's Day in South Africa, I was more than a little embarrassed by my lack of knowledge and even more ashamed by my lack of consciousness.

A question floored my ego, and even more so, my justifications for not knowing found no solid ground whatsoever.

16. "Valentina Trechekova (sic) was the first woman to do what?

    A) Break the sound barrier
    B) Go into space
    C) Reach the South Pole
    D) Summit Mount Everest

I had no clue.

And worse, was that I didn't know a single name of any woman who had accomplished those things, so I couldn't even narrow my odds for a lucky guess. I knew every man though, as the names Chuck Yeager, Yuri Gagarin, Sir Edmund and Amundsen rolled out of the filing systems of the left brain of my male dominated library.

I couldn't say I wasn't born then. All of these feats had been accomplished long before I was born—the last one being Yuri's foray into space in 1961, some eight years before my birth. I could not deny that stories of human endeavour hadn't fascinated me since the day I could pick up a Guinness Book of World Records, let alone read one. I had no excuse for not knowing.

Why were these efforts of men so widely known and celebrated, yet the women who accomplished these extraordinary endeavours were much like the rest of my Sunday Times—largely tossed aside for the recyclers.

As this epiphany of significant realisation sunk in, I thought that these women may well have had far greater hurdles to overcome than even the feats themselves.

How much societal noise would Jackie Cochran have had to endure in her pursuit of breaking the sound barrier? And how many more barriers did she break besides the one of sound amidst many a deaf ear?

Did Ann Bancroft suffer more cold shoulders and frosty receptions from potential funders than the icy weather she overcame to be the first women to have stood at both poles as late as 1993? That is more than eighty years after the well documented race between Scott and Amundsen, meaning that only a handful of people alive when Amundsen won, would still have been alive to witness Bancroft's own triumph.

Was the height of Mount Everest just another step in the journey of a hundred other hurdles which Junko Tabei had to climb to stand tall on the summit of Everest on the 16th May 1975?

Had I known of these three incredible women, I would have known that Valentina Tereshkova was indeed the first woman in space.

I wonder how many closed-minded males she would have met before enjoying the freedom of open space?

In honour of all women in South Africa and beyond. And not just because it's women's month.

(Source: Wikipedia)

What's in a name?

With this question, thoughts immediately take me back to Mr 'Smoothy' Smith's English classes in the mid-nineteen eighties. He was the most easily side-tracked teacher I can remember, and any chance to avoid trying to tutor teenagers through the toil of Shakespearian set works was jumped upon. We had arrived at the famous 'rose' quote, and Smoothy had asked us for metaphor and meaning in this well-known line in which Juliet proclaims her love for Romeo regardless of the sting of his surname.

'Would a rose by any other name smell just as sweet, boys?'

"It depends who Rose is, Sir."

And then a whole lot of inappropriate comments on the poor fictional and fantasy-fuelled Rose would follow, punctuated by the banter of breaking voices and titters of teenage tremors.

"Please Sir, can't you just tell us a joke?"

"You are a joke Robson."

With a wink to the joker to signal his complete lack of malice, and without breaking neither his stride nor his thespian performance, Smoothy sauntered into a story.

Piet Pimplebottom had had enough. Enough of the snide comments behind his back and his bottom. Enough of being the 'butt' of everyone's jokes and their rear end ridicule. He rushed to the department of Home Affairs to change his name the next morning.

He returned to the golf course with a big smile and a fresh outlook on life. He had a new name and a fresh new identity.

'What is your new name now Piet?' they asked.

"It is not Piet. It is Hennie. Hennie Pimplebottom."

And so, the lesson devolved into a different discussion mixed with mirth, and it diffused into confusion. He talked about two dogs he owned. A Basset Hound whose only thing longer than his ears and droopier than his eyes, was his scrotum. He was close to the ground in every way and moved only for food or a new position at the fire. His name was 'Flash.'

The second dog was an English Mastiff, and at well over one hundred kilograms, and struggling to fit through the doorway, was equally inaptly named 'Twinkletoes'.

In a remarkable show of experienced timing, just seconds before the bell rang to signal the end of the lesson, Smoothy left us with an essay question for homework.

"Does your name define your character, or does your character define your name?"

The Penny had dropped. At least I knew a Penny. I hadn't yet met a Rose, and although the bell had rung for the end of the lesson, the learning had only just begun.

Ever since then I have been held intrigued by names. We apparently even prefer the initials of our names to any other letters in the alphabet, and we are more likely to donate to relief efforts of hurricanes which carry the same name as us, or even begin with the same letter. Our names mean something to us, and a name is often the first piece of information we have about someone. Through association and through past experiences, we can make up a whole story about someone at just the mention of their name, and we can do this in a few seconds. A high school bully or an ex-girlfriend. An inspiring mentor, a celebrity or a University crush. A close friend or that neighbour who still owes you money or someone with the same name as your children. All these characters may enter our consciousness in the briefest of moments, and we form instantaneous opinion.

During some recent family ailments and injuries, I had the misfortune of visiting four different hospitals in a shade over a week. They were all under the same company brand, and had the same set of values on the wall for all to see, and hopefully to live by. After greeting, the second value on the chart was:

"I always wear my NAME BADGE to show my identity."

Without exception, the staff at all levels wore their name badges, and in places like hospitals, the ability to connect with someone quickly is often of great importance. If even for a friendly coffee made with love in the hospital eatery. We all know how it feels when someone remembers our name. We feel a boost of energy, and a surge in spirit—a sense that we matter to someone, that we are relevant and that there is significance in our identity. Sometimes I walk into a grocery store after a day of training and I've forgotten to remove my name badge. The cashier greets me by my name, and it stops me in my tracks. I feel worthy and that I belong.

I am sure the world would be a better place if we walked around with our names on our chests and close to our hearts. Our names are close to our hearts, and I am prepared to wager that our behaviour would be far more tempered if we were constantly displaying our names. There might be some subtle accountability, and it would be highly conducive to connecting.

Everyone has a story, and there is some wisdom in the adage that when you know someone's story, you most often see them in a far more positive light. Knowing someone's story leads to more understanding, and more understanding increases tolerance and reduces hate. Our life stories begin with our own names, and in Africa, that name often carries great meaning. If you are Slindile, it means your parents have been waiting, and if your name is Zanele, it means enough; you are unlikely to have younger siblings. The factory is closed.

It is not unusual to find people following the meaning of their names into their professions in a contended resignation and acceptance of their fate that they had no choice. It was simply my name, and therefore my destiny, they might say. I remembered the best golf caddie I probably ever walked with was at Leopard Rock in the Eastern Highlands of Zimbabwe. His name was 'Advance.' There's no better name for a caddie, and his ABC of Attitude, Behaviour, and Character were all about that part of his identity. He will advance in life even if it is barefoot, and especially if it is off the beaten track.

During Lockdown we had an issue with one of our locks. Ironic you would think until you hear the name of the locksmith who arrived on his motorbike and provided us with an essential service. His name? Havelock. You can't script this stuff because in a sense it has been scripted before he was born.

My all-time favourite coffee, 'Bean There', arrives at my house delivered by none other than 'Future' and nothing and no one could be brighter than his smiling face as he heralds an immediately bright future for me with great coffee.

On one of our first evenings out since lockdown has eased was at the Delta Café along the Braamfontein spruit at the western edge of Craighall Park. It was a spectacular meal made even more memorable by the masterful service of 'Masterpiece'. We all think our children are masterpieces, but few parents hand that name over to their children with belief and conviction that they will live into the heritage of their name.

Names carry meaning. They are precious to us in that they are the vehicle of our identity, and sometimes they tell a story. Ask someone their name today, and if you can, ask what it means. You will start a conversation, and conversation by conversation we strengthen community, and maybe we even build a country.

If our heritage is something we inherit, can there be anything more meaningful which we carry with us for our entire lives than our names given to us at birth?

I looked up the meaning of my own name. 'Crown' or 'wreath' came up first which I found totally uninspiring, but in digging a bit deeper, its origins lie in encircling, protecting and including. I now understand why I really love circular conversations around a fire under an African night sky.

Mr. Smith Sir, it has taken me over thirty years to pay proper attention to your question of whether your name defines your character, or your character defines your name. I apologise for my tardiness in handing in a considered response.

(With great thanks to Jeff Thomas aka 'Sthombesejongosi' for the help in translation.)

To understand his name, you simply have to be present. It is a theatrical performance.

And there is dancing involved!

P.S. I ran a webinar for a well-known pharmaceutical on the importance of greetings to establish a connection, a conversation, and hopefully, a long-lasting relationship with their customers. One of the pharmacies listening in from Umhlanga in KZN had t-shirts with their names printed on made for their staff, and an arrow pointing up towards their face, so that their customers would know them even though their faces were hidden by masks.

They told me that the energy was almost tangible. I could feel it even in their voices.

Go on. Greet someone and find out their names.

And be prepared, for Africa is a place of stories.

Question ?!

Pre-thought note:

There is a good reason for the double punctuation mark. When superimposed on one another, the question and the exclamation mark become one. The interrobang was birthed as a result of two different parents, the 'interro' coming from the interrogative question, and the 'bang' being the slang word used by printers from as early as the 1960's (Wikipedia).

The interrobang has elicited some furious debate in libraries and literary circles ever since. One can only imagine the academic aggression being postured at Oxford or Cambridge tea parties against this American imposter of punctuation, (their only one in three hundred years) making its shady and schizophrenic presence palpable. In frustration, a cucumber sandwich was likely tossed with disdain, and the contemptuous comment against its inclusion in the hallowed pages of the English language may well have been:

"Are you serious?!"

"Really?!"

A brave soul at the same gathering may have muttered from the back rows of both their seats and their dentures,

"He just used the interrobang twice Edna. I think we should take it as entrenched."

I like this offspring of two wonderful parents. Imagine having a parent who is deeply questioning; who explores understanding through searching and who asks always if there is a better way forward. Someone who is comfortable in the unknowing and who can sit with the polarities and ambiguities of the explored life. The other parent being a flash of spontaneous excitement filled with emotion. One who lives right in the moment, who appreciates sentiment and who impulsively expresses their feelings.

Diversity breeds new ideas with a statement disguised as a question or vice versa.

Back to the thought:

My daughter arrived home from school one day. She was about six years old at the time. I could see in her sparkling eyes that she had learned something new today, and she had that mischievous look of the learner about to become the teacher.

"Dad, what is the difference between knowledge and wisdom?"

There is such a thing as an immediate pain behind the eyeball, much like an ice cream headache which develops when trying to answer an academic question posed by a six-year-old. I searched hard for an appropriate and brilliant answer, and I failed dismally. How does a father explain this when he doesn't know the answer himself?

Hannah allowed me to sweat through my uncertainty and by the sparkle in her eyes she was relishing this reversal of roles which would increasingly become the norm in our household. Eventually she would put me out the misery of my unknowing.

"Dad, it's OK. I know the answer."

"Knowledge is knowing that a tomato is a fruit. Wisdom is knowing not to put that tomato into a fruit salad."

Ever since that day when I, as the student was ready and the teacher appeared, I have been intrigued by the difference between knowledge and wisdom. Generally, I have quoted Einstein as saying that:

Knowledge is having the right answers. Wisdom lies in asking the right questions.

Through all my recent research, there is no exact tie of these words to Einstein, so perhaps it should be attributed to the greatest philosopher of all time. Anonymous.

What still holds true though is the untapped potential of the question. How many answers might we receive, and will those answers be the same as those regurgitated from last week's management meeting? Could we find ourselves exploring not just the possible answer, but a whole new set of potential relationships? Or might they even deepen the strong relationships we already have? Like a successful gold prospector who surveys the land before panning, a great question might map out the landscape of the thinking, burrow beneath the fearful, crusty dry surface of exposure and tap into the rich vein of vulnerability.

It is in that vein where we find the valuable nuggets, and as the first shy nugget of sharing surfaces, a rush of golden ideas might emerge from the construct of a carefully crafted question.

Earlier on in this journey, I mentioned the poet, Rainer Maria Rilke who in an extract from *Letters to a Young Poet* perhaps provides some advice to us all in our searching:

"Live the questions now. Perhaps then, someday far in the future, you will gradually, without even noticing it, live your way into the answer."

One could go into a full day's workshop to delve into this glorious guidance, and it is something I am still trying hard to do when everything seems to be screaming for a right and reliable answer in these current times of Covid.

There are few things more beautiful for me than a rich example from the world of true stories, and I was uplifted by an all too brief snippet of a good news story which held at its heart a quite magnificent question.

The Bel Aire Diner in Queens New York is a restaurant opened in 1965, and was then bought in 1996 by a Greek-American couple named Archie and Patty Dellaportas. Since that day, it has been open every minute of every day for over twenty-four years. In Ancient Greek parlance, that would be called an Aeon—a broad sweep of time.

When Covid-19 arrived as an unwelcome guest with its devastating feedback form, they did what they could by offering take out, signing up with food delivery apps, and services, and selling vouchers up front. These measures barely kept them afloat, and they were still seventy percent down in sales in a one hundred and eighty-seater eatery. While it might only take three well placed darts to fill "One hundred and eeeeeiiiiiiiigggggghhhhhhtttttyyy" as a perfect score, it takes a whole lot more than that to fill a restaurant and its hungry balance sheet.

And then emerged the golden question.

"How can we bring people in without actually bringing people in?"

Well, to cut to the front of the food queue, The Bel Aire Diner suddenly became the Bel Aire Drive—In.

At Thirty-Two USD per car, tickets are sold on line, and like all great attractions, touts outside the parking lot are turning their own profits. There are no queues for food which is delivered to your vehicle window. Double feature movies—all family friendly, are shown on an inflatable screen. Breakfasts are still made, but donated to the needy, and Oh, if you need the facilities, please just wear a mask.

Sometimes if we look back along the hooked thorn on our Zizyphus branch, we realise that we might already have the answer for which we so desperately search, and maybe we could add to the genius of Rainer Maria Rilke that we might not only "live our way into the answer",

But might we be able to relive our way into our own answer?

The question turns a problem into a challenge and a crisis into an opportunity, or even an infinite set of possibilities.

P.S. That last word is both an invitation and a suggestion.

As in, please question, I would love your comment, and we should question—it keeps us curious.

Leadership Lessons from a Jazz Band

The air here is a thick blanket of smoke. It is a warm smoke made up primarily of smooth cigars and rolled cigarillos and it doesn't seem to have the throat catching nicotine noose which might cause a hacking carbonised cough. Hints of cherry tobacco, mocha and crème de menthe almost lie in layers like a well poured Irish coffee and the feeling of quiet conviviality could be Eastern European. It is not the boisterous Gaelic type of folk dancing, Guinness glugging gregariousness, and neither is it the sombre stare over a dram filled Scottish Quaich with a silent gaze back over the links of remorse and regret.

We have found this place purely by accident, and fortuitous accidents are often a product of an open mind, an absent agenda and a willing awareness. The art and the science of tracking is not something you'd usually associate with the beautiful Danish city of Copenhagen with its centuries old and worn cobbled streets, but tracking is not only about looking and seeing with fresh eyes, it is also about hearing through uncluttered ears—and what is wafting gently through the air of the midnight sun has caught our attention. Much like the ratcheting sound of ox peckers in the bush heightens the awareness on the trail, our interest is piqued towards the promise of more pub than pachyderm.

Our pace quickens as the musical fly lines embedded into our earlobes becomes taught and we are reeled in, and almost past, the entrance to the HVIDE LAM. With only three small tables outside and a modest, non-descript doorway, it is easily missed. The fly lines in our right ears jerk us like a well-played trout back towards the source of the music and into a net of contentment.

We peer into a small space with a huge atmosphere, and our calculations of "THE WHITE LAMB" being no bigger than around forty square metres were confirmed by the presence of the smoke through which we were peering. You see, if your establishment is this size or smaller, then smoking is permitted in this strange land. Anything larger, and your lungs have constitutionally enforceable rights. Having grown up in a household where my mother smoked—and my wife used to—smoke has never bothered me. Besides, there was something far more influential on the senses which hit us with a velvet glove.

A full five-piece jazz band was at play—and I mean at play, and not at work. No doubt they were working hard at their craft and in so doing, they were delighting their customers, but the overall sense was one of play as they jammed together through an organised chaos of collaboration. The musicians were as unique as their instruments and one could only wonder at how each of their stories brought them together in a forty square metre pub on the square of Kultorvet, Copenhagen where the sign above the bar reads 1807. Collectively their musical experience could comfortably have been over two hundred years itself, and the double bassist would be lucky to pass for twenty with a fake ID. Looking resentfully like Matt Damon with a God given musical talent, he would hit the neck with all his young fingers could offer and pluck the strings above the bridge in a perfect display of pizzicato. When he played solo, he frowned intently towards the musical notes of the pianist, but when he could free up his left hand whilst still keeping a rhythm with his right, he would glug with great gusto from a bottle of beer. His fingers equally adept on the neck of the bottle as they were on the neck of the bass. It seemed his only challenge lay in keeping the sea horse shaped scroll of the double bass from bashing against the Tuborg sponsored speakers and the Oxford green lamp shades emitting their low light over the wooden panelling.

The pianist was the only woman in this ensemble and maybe because of this fact, she never stopped smiling. Not once. Whether she tinkered or tippled there was always the sweet smile of someone who knew what they were doing, and maybe more importantly, why they were doing it. She could have been Matt Damon's Granny, and one could easily picture her in a country garden tending seasonal flowers or gathering berries in a basket. One could easily imagine her as a small-town librarian, but a librarian never too far away from a glass of crisp chardonnay.

On the far right, and closest to the ladies' toilet was the Tenor Sax. Pale and grey, the product of many long and harsh Danish winters, with burgundy red lips made for the saxophone and probably just as useful on the clarinet as on the rim of a full-bodied claret. Perhaps the inventor of this remarkable instrument, Adolphe Sax, had this type of character in mind when he dreamed up this musical resonation. He wore a spotlessly polished badge of his own instrument proudly on his lapel, and he seemed never to stop a constant nodding of approval—at the music, towards his fellow band members, and what became abundantly obvious, at the audience.

With the best line of sight to the entrance and the ladies loo, he was often the first to notice a new guest or a familiar face, and, as I will share, played a crucial role of connection in the customer energy of the evening. It would not be surprising to see this gent announcing each and every player as the starter of the Open Championship on the windswept links of coastal Scotland, and the ripples of applause at the end of every announcement meant for the player would be humbly and generously deflected to the other players in this band—and of course to the music itself.

We would learn during the evening that this jolly jazz band would have no leader—but they would have a coordinator. Someone who booked the venues and called the team together, and maybe suggested the song sheet. In everything he seemed non-descript and could have passed as an understated English teacher at an above average school. He smiled, but not too much. He sipped, but never a lot, and he played, but gave more space than he occupied. With a neatly trimmed beard and dull, dark framed spectacles as square as the setting of his jaw he looked strangely lost without a lectern, and if he wasn't a teacher, the next stereotypical guess might have been a priest. His approach was measured and perhaps his air of control might inspire a confidence that things would not fall apart. He was undoubtedly professional, and we would learn that he was indeed a full-time musician. You don't become this accomplished at the Alto Sax by standing behind a lectern or in front of a power point presentation.

The last, or so we thought at the time, member of the band was seated with his back against the side of the piano, and the only thing which would have made his life easier would have been a well-oiled swivel chair enabling him to remain connected to the unwritten threads and nuances of his craft. He played the banjo, and could almost have played it with the sparkle in his eyes alone. He looked elfish and with his tinsel-coloured mop of steel wool hair, one could be forgiven in thinking that somewhere a Christmas tree is missing a prized decoration. I could have sworn that he played the part of one of Robin Hood's merry men, and lived in Nottingham forest. He may not have been the leader either, but it sure felt like he was the glue—and as a carpenter by day, I am sure he would feel comfortable with that analogous appreciation. I wondered if he had children—for if he does, they would be blessed at night by lullabies and bestowed with wooden toys during the day. I am sure he makes magnificent furniture, but I am prepared to bet my next expensive Tuborg beer that his first love would be to make toys.

And so, we watched as these five musical maestros weaved a web of entertainment from their fingers and their mouths, and as we watched, we listened, and as we listened, we learned. Something jazz musicians do as a matter of course.

If there was a great metaphor to apply in today's increasingly complex world, and a way through it, I think jazz bands could teach us a thing or two. There is of course some structure and total agreement around the piece to be played, but it seems as though no particular piece is ever played in exactly the same way twice. Each performance is unique. There is a huge invitation here towards playing out of who you are being in the moment, and to play with individual expression, innovation and improvisation.

Far more enlightening though than any structure, is the space offered within it. Not many people walking into a new house comment on the beauty of the walls, they are taken by the comfort in the spaces between those walls. What these team members were offering to each other more than anything else was a space to play into. Yes, a safe space where they had an idea of where to play, but also a place in which to risk and to push themselves and to explore—or not to, and hand it back to the next member whilst taking a bottled breather.

It seems so simple. Give others space to shine, to express themselves, to run free and take risks and in so doing to learn whilst playing, and as they do so, keep them in the zone with the odd tap or tinkle or a clicked finger correction to show support. Each one relished the opportunity to go solo—but none of the team left the room or the music. From solo to support and back to solo, and the support is shown with a nod of appreciation and encouragement as much as it is with a plucked chord or a pressed key.

Maybe most importantly, every customer was delighted, and it started with every one of us being acknowledged. With each new entrant there was a nod or a wink and most certainly a smile, and as happens with things infectious, there was contagion. The nods and winks and smiles were returned and were reinvested into the entertainment. They were playing for their customers and they were playing for fun!

As much as these five were diversely eclectic, so too were their audience. There were young investment banking types in ties and builders in boots. Leather jackets were as popular as leggings and all types of hair, from bald heads and beards like ZZ Top, to the quintessential Scandinavian blonde were carefully coiffed or left uncombed. Some came here to lose themselves, others maybe to find themselves. Either way the result was probably in their favour.

At a point in the twilit evening, the room darkened significantly, yet it was still light outside. The railway sleeper framed door was open, but the way was closed, and if the smoke only had forty square metres to waft around in before, it was about to have a whole lot less.

Crammed into a tight yellow cardigan and billowing out in a large blue tent, this latest and by far biggest patron somehow managed to squeeze her way in towards the central table. In the colours of the Swedish flag, she may well have been able to warmly envelop a large part of that entire country with the amount of material on display.

The knitted beanie was removed, and along with it our suspicions were confirmed that this was indeed Obelix's identical twin sister. Two long python sized plaits of ginger hair tumbled towards the table, and to give this throwback to the Viking era some benefit of the doubt, we assumed that the large signature stone carried by her brother in the comic strips was still concealed under the blue marquee. On peering out of the street level window

there was indeed no evidence of a menhir. Many concrete blocks to stop the horrific trend of suicide trucks, but no visible tall, upstanding stone.

As tables were moved and a seemingly inadequate stool was found, the band never broke stride. This was just another customer to delight, and by set three, she was nothing short of delighted. With drumstick sized thumbs and frankfurter fingers she thumped away at the beat. Her pigtails of plaits might have caused serious bodily harm to the frail old Indian gent nearby as they swung like wrecking balls not altogether in time with the rhythm, and the largest of smiles just beamed broader.

It was that smile which changed our pictures of this woman. Before its emergence one would have paid avoidance money to her in a dark alley. In its presence she was just another human being and a fellow lover of jazz.

Whilst our assumptions and viewpoints were challenged and changed throughout the evening, her small three-legged stool, though splayed like a giraffe's legs during a long drink of water or a well walked golfers stand bag, thankfully held firm, and as one round turned to two, and then three, and then who-really-cares-how-many, so too did the band keep morphing in a Protean sort of way.

This God of rivers and oceanic bodies of water from Greek Mythology could tell the future to anyone who asked, but the trick was that he could change his shape or his form to avoid having to do that. Anyone who could catch him, would have power beyond their imagination. The problem was, he was uncatchable.

And so too, in a way was this jazz band. It could change form, and suddenly, after a moment's quiet consultation, there would appear a new pianist. Straight out of the audience, he would replace the gardening librarian and Granny to Matt Damon, and play seamlessly without a note of music. Then a vocalist, on her way to the ladies' loo and close enough to be hugged by the tenor sax on her way past would be given the microphone, the song and the key and we were transported towards a different answer of the future. We would move worlds from Peggy Lee with her caffeine coated voice of 'Black Coffee' to Diana Krall's sultry seductions of 'Just the way you are'. She too was straight out of the crowd and on her way to the bathroom, but close your eyes, and you'd be 'crying a river' with Ella Fitzgerald, and indeed with the streets still alive with the midnight sun, it was undoubtedly 'Summertime' with Billie Holiday.

Individual. Impromptu. Innovative. Yet without the support of the team, the individuals would just be separate isolated soloists.

You simply cannot script evenings like this, except that perhaps they've been going on in this same pub for well over two-hundred years. You just have to be in the right place at the right time with a willingness to explore.

Much like life.

We went in with the intention to have 'one standing up', but ended up seated at the prime table next to the piano for considerably longer than that. It is what happens in smoky jazz clubs in Copenhagen on a Sunday night.

We nodded our appreciation on departure. We received smiles and acknowledgement in return as is customary here.

Thank You. Pleasure. Such simple things as two more relighted customers found their way back to their homes, and themselves, in the light of the night.

And relighted is not a typo.

Green Shoots

At the end of winter 2019, we have a lot to be negative about. And not just in South Africa. Europe has no clue, Britain has no plan, and the US, it would seem, has no morals. If there was a single country doing well right now, their celebration will be short term, because listening to the news on global climate change, it would appear as though Earth has no future.

Even Johannesburg's saving grace, the trees, are under threat, and the world's largest man- made urban jungle is being condemned to a slow death by a miniscule migrant from South East Asia. On my street alone, large red bandages of plastic doom strangle the stems of London Planes and English Oaks, as these once proud trees stand barren and bare and sentenced to the saw of the next municipal undertaker. It is a depressing procession of red gloom, and the big letters written read PSHB. The Polyphagous Shot Hole Borer Beetle is spreading throughout South Africa like a cancer, and it seems as though, just like the state of the rest of the world, there is no known cure.

"Perhaps the truth depends on a walk around a lake."

These words by the poet Wallace Stevens have always walked with me when I feel that I have no answers, and although I was under no illusion of finding some big answers to the world's massive challenges, I was pleasantly surprised by what I found as I left the single bounded truth of my own walls of worry. The air was summery, warm and almost hazy, and what struck me was the abundant birdsong in the suburbs. During winter, my mind had run amok with thoughts of dead trees meaning no birds, yet here they were, and they were announcing their presence loudly. My eyes turned up towards many of the branches of the red labelled condemned trees, and I saw more green leaves than I had thought possible. There were still many dead looking branches, but in some cases half the tree was bearing shiny new leaves, and on other trees, new shoots had sprouted from the thickest of boughs, and even from the most stubborn and gnarled of trunks.

It seemed almost as if the tree has found a way to survive. It has prioritised its energy, sacrificed some of the old structures, and found avenues of new growth, however difficult. I wondered if there weren't some great lessons right there for my own life?

Could I let go of some of the clutter of old ways and accumulations, and grow some exciting new possibilities? Could I be sure of putting my own energy into the real things which matter, and not cast this precious resource into the abyss of anxiety?

Perhaps there is a message here for our own Government? The old structures are in need of pruning, and the tree does this from within. There is still an energy in the tree, and it is desperately looking for a new path, and while it may not be the same massively abundant provider of shade which it once was, it will grow if allowed and flourish if encouraged.

Wallace Stevens never learned to drive, and composed all of his poetry whilst walking. He escaped the single version of the truth one often finds from behind a desk with a looped news channel on in the background.

With a fresh perspective on my next walk, perhaps I could see the 'wood' for the trees? Now, whilst I can't verify this entirely, I have learned from a wise mentor that the original statement that we "can't see the wood for the trees", may indeed be flawed. The word 'Wold' is an Old English meaning of a clearing, or 'an elevated, treeless tract of land' according to Your Dictionary.com, and it would make sense then that we can't see the clearing for the trees as an interpretation of this well-known phrase.

A piece of that forest of assumption was removed from my own eye when I met William on my latest walk around the hallowed turf of a golf course—where it seemed as though I made acquaintance with most of its trees.

William arrived neatly attired in his white caddy overall. His face still smiled through a nasty looking gash to his top lip and across the bridge of his nose. It looked painfully recent. Immediately I put up my red banner of censure and jumped into judgement. Caddy. Weekend. Liquor. Barfight. Shame, life is tough for some. Like the trees of Johannesburg, he stands no chance.

There was something though about the spring in his step which was like a green shoot of possibility through the mindset of the probable. I asked him what had actually happened.

His eyes lit up. Rugby injury. Flank forward for Blanco Rugby team. Try saving tackle. Boot in the face.

There are millions of Williams in our country, and all we want to hear is the term 'Green Shoots'. Through all the clutter and chaos of his own life, he knows what to do. Cut away that which doesn't serve, prioritise your own energy, and focus on the job in the moment.

I would have loved to have seen that tackle.

It may have closed one of his eyes temporarily, but it opened both of mine as I saw William not through a lens of superiority, but rather through one of uniqueness.

Sarvodaya -Wellbeing for All

This is the name of Mahatma Gandhi's house. The one in KwaZulu Natal, South Africa, on the outskirts of Phoenix nestled amongst the bustling settlement of Bhambayi. It was burned down in 1985 in the wake of the politically charged Inanda riots, but has been rebuilt and now serves as a largely undiscovered haven of hospitality in an informal sprawl of Humanity.

Our times here are special and sometimes even spiritual, and it provides a space to eat, talk and breathe at a slower pace after the sensory assault of the weekend.

The surrounding community was settling into its Sunday afternoon routines, and as I watched the ritual of weekly washing, I wondered at how Gandhi himself might have sat on the veranda of the Indian Opinion printing press and gazed over the drastically different scene in front of him over a century ago. What would have been subsistence farming then is now a patchwork pattern of makeshift shelters cobbled together with cables and corrugated iron.

An old Gogo—the affectionate term for grandmother—was doing her washing in four shallow plastic tubs and in each one stood a small child stomping out the stains and squeezing the soapy water into every filthy fibre of fabric. Whilst work was taking place, a game was emerging simultaneously, and there was clearly more fun to have four little feet dancing on the denim, and then six, and then all eight, as the leader hopped from one hurdle to another.

A steeplechase ensued and as the waters frothed, the bubbles became snow white beards, and the slippery suds would slide over the edge and lap over into the dusty sand like the stormy seas of a choppy ocean.

As toes became entwined in trousers, there would be spills of the human kind too, and with each fall the hilarity would rise—and with each recovery more mud would end up in the washing than out.

The old Gogo just smiled. Perhaps she was thinking, there will always be next Sunday.

When the menial and mundane turns to muddy magic through imagination, something supernatural is at play, and watching life unfold in this way is simply enchanting.

When purpose is present, good work happens and when the purpose is play, engagement is natural.

The process may be muddy at first, but nothing which a sheet of reject wrapping won't sort out for next Sunday's washing ritual.

Changing a chore to a chortle swings a scowl to a smile and Grandchildren influence their Grandparents.

I wonder how often I see some of the work I do as a necessary evil to reach the other side, when perhaps just getting there would be far more fun in the play.

If leadership comes in multiple shapes and sizes, then so too, does influence. When the honey-eyed stare of a large lioness causes Land Cruisers to part like the Red Sea under Moses' instruction, we are physically, emotionally, and maybe even spiritually moved. Without a single sound.

And when a gecko drops in on a conference conversation, pandemonium ensues as tables and chairs scatter, drinks are spilled, and fully-grown men and women spread as if flung from an overturned vehicle at high speed.

Imagine the family talk at the geckoes' household that evening...

"How did you cause all that panic, Dad? You left a wake of destruction, escaped capture, and no one slept through Mick's lecture. How did you do all that?"

"I'm not sure, my boy. I dropped in on a conversation...."

He (or she) was not trying to be a lion or an elephant or even a snake. Just a gecko being a gecko.

Authentic leadership moves followers to alter the course of the moment. Gandhi shifted a nation and geckos shift furniture. A look from a lion levers Land Cruisers, and children can change adult mindsets. A young female leopard stops the clock of our measured world while she laps up water as her impossibly long whiskers dance in dryness and the gently raised hand of a Ranger refashions the route of the largest of all land mammals.

We influence through our being. And perhaps in that we are indeed equipotent.

Sarvodaya—"wellbeing for all".

Not doing.

Being. And the journey of who we are being is our own unique journey

P.S.

What an authentic act of Humanity displayed by our President in the donning of his mask in front of the nation a couple of days ago.

In what could have been an embarrassing moment, he laughed at himself and with others the next day, as opposed to laughing at others by himself.

Perhaps we are most significantly influenced through authenticity. When mistakes are not masked and pretences are unprotected.

We see the real, and isn't that so much easier to follow?

Choice

The car was being put through its paces and was revving high. The excessive speed with which it was moving through the suburbs caused walkers to weave closer to the sidewalks and cyclists to fall into an unusual single file formation. A stop street had been treated merely as a suggestion, and the speed hump down Smits Road had seemingly served no purpose whatsoever.

There were more than a few looks of indignation from the exercising residents and the odd hand signal to encourage a slowing down, but the blur was too fast even for words. I was left speechless by the speed of the unlicensed car.

The gears ground down as a rally car would into the corner, and with no hint of hesitation the vehicle was flung right into Christofferson accompanied by a squealing of tyres pushed to their road holding limitations.

It was then that I saw the whites of their eyes. A blind form of panic was written in their wide-open eyes.

Whilst all around them were walking or running, the occupants of this vehicle were clearly on the run.

Just a few days before, our gate buzzer had rung gently. It seems strange to say the word 'gently', as to my knowledge there is no volume control from the button outside the gate, but it was almost polite—just like the first few vibrations of an African Scops Owl's call, and it was only pressed once. During lockdown, there has understandably been an increase in traffic of the most vulnerable of our society, and there have been a number of deliveries to the gate of food parcels or left overs. Sometimes in the desperate hope for attention, the button is held down for extended periods, or pushed repeatedly, and every now and then all buttons are pushed causing a kind of Mexican wave cacophony which reverberates through all sections of the house.

The soft 'prrrrp' was a welcome relief, and I took a moment to observe the young man on the other side of the security camera before I answered the intercom phone. It was Friday, but he was dressed in his Sunday best. Sporting a jacket and tie, polished shoes and a student like book sack slung over his shoulder, he had his mouth close to the receiver as if he was about to deliver an address.

He might as well have, because the voice which followed could make him famous on radio. He was beautifully spoken, with an engaging edge and a trimming of humour and hope.

He was here to sell books, and my unfettered assumption was that they were religious books. I asked him to wait while I fetched my remote control and marched with a degree of self-irritation as to why I had disallowed myself the choice of saying No. There are many in my family who would rightly label me as a born sucker—this would no doubt be the latest piece of dinnertime evidence to be repeated at length and with mirth at my expense.

Well-schooled in the new Covid way of greeting, Craig Kanyemba offered me the pointed part of his bent elbow, along with one of the brightest smiles and set of shining eyes I can remember seeing. Perhaps I hadn't seen too many of these rare features due to lock down, and perhaps I had missed these human interactions so immensely that now, upon receiving them, I felt like the starving man who is happy with stale bread.

My children would say that I have the capacity to cut a short story long—another dinner time jibe mentioned when I sail into the explanation of anything I feel passionate about, so to eliminate that for now:

I bought three books.

Craig Kanyemba had authored these himself. If it wasn't for lockdown, there would be another three available, but they had been stalled at the printers. He is a Zimbabwean and lives at Gandhi Square, only metres from where we take leadership groups on immersions to learn about life. He studies computer science at Unisa, and he writes to put himself through his own education.

He is not yet twenty-four years old.

An extract from his book *Against All Odds: A Road to USA*, reads as follows:

"A lesson from Nature; Zebras do not look at Tigers and wish they could hunt like Tigers. Accept yourself as you are, know your weaknesses and strengths and embrace your unique beauty and gifts. The universal law of correspondence; Most of us have heard the adage that our outer world is nothing more than a reflection of our inner world—as within, so without, as above, so below."

The young author and philosopher walked off with the spring of self-achievement in his step, and a smile without swagger. I left with three books downloaded onto my phone and a bunch of new reading material for lockdown.

In the course of one's life there are sometimes quotes or stories, pieces of writing or poems which stick with you, and occasionally they become a companion in the quiet or a friend you introduce around the fire. Like a great memory they might remain dormant for a long period of time, but like a great relationship, they almost seem to spontaneously re-combust with the lightest of a catalytic caress. From a far-flung fissure in the deep recess of recollection, I remember a haunting yet humbling piece of poetry from a time and place far worse than what most of us are going through during lockdown.

"From tomorrow on I shall be sad

Not today.

Today I will be glad,

And every day, no matter how bitter it may be,

I shall say,

From tomorrow on, I shall be sad,

Not today."

Apparently from a child in a Nazi death camp

What is it that causes one white eyed youngster to be running from his past, and another to be whistling towards his future? One leaves damage and destruction, the other leaves only dignity. Reckless or respectful. Hopeless or hopeful.

Leadership is about choice. We choose to lead, or we choose not to lead. Life is all about choice too, I guess. We choose to steal, or we choose to write books. We choose to engage with an intercom call, or we elect to waive the opportunity away.

I look forward to meeting Craig again, perhaps for a coffee in Gandhi Square, and learning how much someone more than half my age could teach me about a different life. I wish I had written six books—even at the age of fifty—but maybe that is akin to the zebra wanting to hunt like a tiger.

Because I have his cell phone number, I will choose to do just that. A coffee with Craig Kanyemba.

P.S. Multiple coffees later, and with the wisdom and guidance of my much younger mentor, the outcome is the book you are now reading.

Who would have thought?

POLARITY 6

DO POWER AND AUTHORITY GET THINGS DONE, OR COULD ENERGY AND INFLUENCE GET THINGS DONE?

The higher goal in this last chapter is to enjoy 'fully charged' engagement.

RED VIEW OF MORE TENSION:

Power and authority get things done.

"If all you have is a hammer, everything looks like a nail."

Abraham Maslow

I have no doubt that if any of us were in an emergency landing, we would want the pilot to take full control of the situation. We would be told what to do and we would do as we're told. Powerful people shut down economies during a pandemic, and we obey the uniformed police officer when they ask us to pull over. There is a place for power, for control, for clear consequences, and a strong rule of law. But if this is the only view we possess, we use this hammer to smash everything which looks even remotely like a nail. While nails were made to be hammered, human beings were not, and I think we are seeing a world rising up against the use of power by the powerful over the powerless.

For the sake of clarity, when I talk about 'Power', I am referring to top down, hierarchical, autocratic, manipulative power over others. Command and control. An authority over others because of rank or title or financial control. I am not talking of the positive power we feel from within, or the power of emotions, or the powerful impact which a positive influence can have in our lives. These can all be immensely beneficial to us, but I wonder if we have lived for such a long time with this mindset that the unconsidered use of power over others has become a natural default position?

Is there an alternative approach which will help achieve things?

BLUE VIEW TOWARDS CONNECTION:

Energy and Influence get things done.

In every leadership experience I have had the privilege of facilitating over twenty-five years, a simple analogy has always emerged:

You can own a million-dollar motor car, but if the battery is flat, it is useless to you as a mode of transport.

In our own lives, a spark of energy gets us to go for a run, to read a book, to phone a lead. We have the skills to write a report, but it takes energy to pick up the pen. Last night, as I write, Liverpool Football Club, arguably the greatest team in the world over 2019 and 2020, got thumped seven goals to two by Aston Villa in the English Premier League. You cannot easily argue that they don't have the skills. They have skills in abundance. Perhaps their multi-million Sterling vehicle simply had no charge in the battery during that game?

Energy gets things done. Just ask the 2019 Springbok World Cup winning team, or any other championship winner in any sport for that matter.

As you will read through the stories which follow, along with energy, influence also gets things done. People without title or any positional power or authority can change a situation, a mindset, or even the world. Although there are the undeniable icons of Mahatma Gandhi and Mother Theresa to look up to in this regard, let's go and meet some of the ordinary, everyday people who live amongst us and show us all that influence comes in multiple shapes and forms.

In this chapter we will buy a newspaper from the smiling Bongani and we will leave our car with Christian Kabwe who sees more with his one eye than most of us see with two. We will visit Mam' Khanyi who has mothered over ten thousand children off the streets with the energy of her being, and we will play golf with Aaron the caddy, who has learned to carry his high fives in his heart. We will go to Ellis Park Rugby stadium and meet a young man who kept his crowd in rapturous engagement as he made magic out of the mundane, and we will learn of the importance of followers, not only leaders in effecting change. Next, we will drive through the manic streets of Accra in Ghana, and be led by Michael Marfo on his motorcycle while he conducts a city's traffic on his own, without a wailing siren and flashing blue light. Lastly, we will sit with Blessing, who continues to influence her community of Bhambayi in KZN, SA from within and who has inspired some spontaneous poetry!

If I 'SEE' the importance of energy and influence, my 'DO' might be to lead from where I am with what I have. The 'GET' might just be 'fully charged' engagement.

"Do what you can, with what you have, where you are."

Theodore Roosevelt

Service with a Smile on the Side

Anyone born up to the early 1970's and having lived in Johannesburg will remember the old House of Sports Cars. It was an iconic place on the corner of Jan Smuts and 7th Avenue and it was used as a guide for giving directions—often as a starting point for any destination within five kilometres. These memorable places were important reference points, and even many years after it closed down, it was always mentioned as a kind of pre-google maps or 'Waze' trig beacon. Children of all ages and from all over Johannesburg would gather to gawk through the glass at the latest Magnum PI model Ferrari, or Bond Aston Martin.

I went often because so did my father.

Just one set of traffic lights down 7th Avenue into Parktown North, on the corner of 7th and 3rd Avenue lives another icon. (You would think some town planner would have made one direction a 'road' and the opposite axis an 'avenue', but perhaps this just adds to the enchanting quirkiness of what is known as 'The Parks' in Jo'burg lingo.)

I was told in glowing terms about this man over a Saturday night drink at a young friends' birthday party, and as the sharer of this story, her radiance grew with every word. The impact this man has had on her all too regular time in the traffic made her large eyes expand even more with the hint of emotional moisture, and when she spoke about the lessons he had taught her children, she lit up with an even wider and abundantly enthusiastic smile.

Being a Sunday, and needing my half dozen chicken samosas from Fournos, and Motherland cappuccino, I travelled way out of my comfort zone to find this inspirational fellow. Bongani sells newspapers, and along with the chilli and caffeine boosts for the body, the puzzle page of the Sunday Times provides me with motivation for the mind. Without one of these three pillars, Sundays are not quite the same. The lady with the smiling eyes from the evening before said I would find him here as he is there every day; she told me to look out for his smile.

I noticed him from a hundred metres away. It did not seem possible that I would encounter two such engaging smiles in less than twelve hours, yet there he was, dancing gently on the painted line between opposing traffic flows like a young gymnast on the beam. With one arm cradling his papered wares, the other one is available for a quick transaction in a Johannesburg second, which is the infinitesimally small synapse of time between a green light and the first blast of an impatient hooter from behind. When not in a transfer of equal value paper on the run through a half open window, the same free arm gestures in a relationship building wave as the cars fly past.

Bongani knows the line between a transaction and a relationship. Many more cars will drive past than will stop or even slow down to buy from him, but perhaps, one day, someone will drive out of their comfort zone by a few hundred metres, roll down a window with the fresh smells of samosas and coffee, and become a new customer. His wave and his smile are his marketing, and his PR, and his customer centric after sales service, all rolled into one.

Danny Meyer is a New York City restauranteur and CEO of the Union Square Hospitality Group. Among many other well established eating houses, he owns The Gramercy Tavern which has been consistently rated as New York's favourite restaurant. In an inspiring You Tube clip, he emphasises 'favourite' over 'best'. If you say something is the best, there is a potential argument over the ratings, the evaluations, the value for money, the quality of the food, the level of service, the neatness of the tables—even the ambience of the lighting. However, if something is your favourite, there is an emotional attachment which cannot be argued.

Meyer proposes that the difference lies in something he calls HQ. Hospitality quotient. It is the way you are made to feel. It is all about the relationship and not just the transaction.

I doubt whether Bongani has ever heard of Danny Meyer, but for over fifteen years this humble migrant labourer from Greyton, KwaZulu Natal has inherently practiced what Meyer is still trying to teach. He has seen a lot of restaurants on this corner come and go, and one meal at any one of them for a single patron could be worth more than he makes in a week. Through rain and shine and the general negativity of each new batch of sensational headlines he carries around every day, he greets his world through the warmth of his being, and he keeps his three children in school.

Leadership is about influence, and the lessons of resilience and relationships, of hard work and of hospitality permeate through the panes and the panels of the passing traffic as generations of young school goers learn the lessons of life.

Not from the newspapers themselves, but rather through the seller.

When I left with my newspaper and my new perspective, I was reminded of the words of Maya Angelou, an American poet and civil rights activist.

"I've learned that people will forget what you said, people will forget what you did, but people will never forget how you made them feel."

Maya Angelou

There are thousands of newspaper sellers who sell exactly the same printed product at precisely the same price, and even with the same pale blue wrapping plastic, but I have a new favourite newspaper seller, and I look forward already to next Sunday.

And it is so in my new comfort zone.

P.S. Perhaps I chose the wrong title for this reflection. The smile is sometimes the main course of service, not just a side dish.

The Seeing Eye

There was a legendary character in the world of South African retail by the name of Ernst Loebenberg. He would scour the stores of Woolworths for men's size sixteen and a half white collared shirts, and his neatly pressed white glove would leak the secrets of any residual dust on the shelves. Dirt was just another piece of valuable information to this fastidious shopkeeper, and as each speck was unshelved by the white fibres of his glove, he would never miss the opportunity to gather insights from his stakeholders. No one was left without a greeting and questions continually flowed, merging together around one single purpose.

The customer.

Born in 1920, living through the Great Depression and then fleeing Germany and the Nazi regime, he arrived in South Africa as a young Jewish teenager. Maybe he developed this ability to pay such close attention to detail because of his background, but perhaps he already had it, and it allowed him to survive in his VUCA world of Volatility, Uncertainty, Complexity and Ambiguity. Sometimes we think these acronyms are recent constructs of our modern world when perhaps they have been around long before David took detailed aim at his Goliathan challenge.

A journey such as this picks up some stories along the way, and Ernst, or Mr. Loebenberg, as even his superiors would often call him, had a book full of these. On one occasion, he dropped off a pie and a drink with his driver Fred, and asked him to wait while he popped back into the Woolworths store from which he had brought it. Being more than a little peckish at the time, Fred tucked into the pie with great relish and was glowing in the spontaneous generosity of his Uber Boss when Mr. Loebenberg bustled back, hunched into the wind of an Adderley Street Cape Doctor and issued Fred with an instruction.

He was to please take this pie to the laboratory to have it tested. A customer had complained that it was off. With the pastry still fresh on his lips, Fred told the truth with chicken-scented breath as he knew that this man would follow up on the results of the food test.

There is not much more to this story, as not much more was said between the Director and the Driver as both travelled in trepidation as to what might happen next. Some loose assumptions had led to some tight muscles, but thankfully Fred's job remained as secure as his bowel. Mr. Loebenberg loved the truth, and he would search for it in people as much as he found it in counting exactly thirteen stitches to the inch in his garments.

Long after his retirement and many years after his death in 2002, The Seeing Eye is a phrase repeated often in the board rooms and training centres of Woolworths.

Helen Keller said, "The only thing worse than being blind is having sight but no vision."

This author, lecturer and political activist was the first blind and deaf person to earn a Bachelor of Arts degree, and she makes a strong point about sight and vision.

Sight is seeing what is. Vision is questioning what could be.

Sight is the tree in front of you. Vision is the low cut with an open blade four iron around the tree to the green. Reality vs possibility, and possibility needs a seeing eye.

Maybe this seeing eye exists in every field of awareness?

Good accountants will see a decimal point in a minefield of numbers, and a great tracker will see the mark of a lightly dragged quill of a porcupine. A caring teacher picks up on a slightly off-colour scholar, and a wide-awake fielder twists impossibly in mid-air and throws down the stumps at the wrong end to alter the course of a five-day test in the blink of his seeing eye.

My sight stops at a brick wall, whereas a great designer envisions the spaces and potential beyond the walls. I see plaster, she sees possibility.

In all walks of life, we park our cars out of routine in the places where we have always parked them, and it sometimes takes a new delegate with fresh eyes to gently comment that perhaps it spoils the view.

When the seeing eye is opened, cars are moved quickly.

It happened to be in a car park in the city of Johannesburg where I received my latest lesson in this remarkable ability we all have, and it left me wondering how often I engage this ability. How many times do I suffer the scotoma of a missed opportunity, or a silent cry for attention from my children?

Too often for sure, but back to the Dunkeld parking lot for now.

My wife and I needed to swap cars and we met in the busy suburban centre of the Dunkeld shops just off Jan Smuts avenue. She had arrived earlier for a hair treatment, and I met her an hour later, whilst still covered in tin foil and resembling a modern-day Christmas tree decoration. We exchanged keys, I left her to her magazines and WhatsApp groups and I walked towards her car. No sooner had I opened the doors with the remote, when a polite question stopped me in my tracks.

"Is this your car, Sir"?

On a Saturday morning in Dunkeld, there is a massive turnover of cars. It is bustling, and in amongst it all stands a car guard who has noticed that the person who parked this car is not the same as the one taking it away.

Christian Kabwe has made it all the way from the DRC to the Dunkeld parking lot, and he has quite a story to tell. He has more computer literacy than many of our current Government ministers are literate full stop. He is a mechanical designer and draughtsman who has also lectured in mathematics, thermal engines and hydro-pneumatic transmission whatever that is, and he loves classical music.

Christian also has only one eye.

But he sees more with that eye than most of us do with two.

A Home full of Hope

Everyone has a story.

In some there are short stories in others a novel, and a rare few should have an entire series written about them. This is a reflection which I should have written some time ago. I have not done so because I have not deemed myself worthy to try and capture in words such an astounding life story as Mam' Khanyi, founder of The Home of Hope.

I remember a story from my youth of a young woman walking down a beach. There were millions of starfish which had washed up from the sea during an unseasonal and maybe unexpected high tide. With the sun baking down and the waters receding to the low points of their natural rhythms, the future of the stranded sea stars looked grim, and a gory genocide would befall this galaxy.

The young woman bends down, picks up a starfish and throws it like a frisbee back into the waiting waves. She takes a few more paces, stares out to the ocean in contemplation, bends down and repeats the process with every few silent strides. An old man is walking towards her and he watches with an increasing interest as he approaches. She is naturally beautiful and he has always been curious, and so there is more than one reason to stop and enquire about her actions.

"Why do you do this?" He asks. "There are millions of them washed up, how on earth do you think you will make a difference?"

She winks at him—this is my version of the story—bends down to pick up another sea creature, and throws it athletically back into waters.

"Well, I made a difference to that one," she smiles and wanders off into the setting sun.

I finally met that lady. Not on an outer beach, but in the inner city, and she wasn't saving starfish, she was saving street children.

For twenty years Mam' Khanyi has been lovingly picking up those who only wished they were beaten by the sun, or left alone on a beach somewhere. She has cared for them and accommodated them. She has nurtured and nourished them, and no amount of writing could capture her levels of love nor the hoops she has jumped through to give them hope.

> *"Love recognises no barriers. It jumps hurdles, leaps fences, penetrates walls to arrive at its destination full of hope."*
>
> *Maya Angelou*

If no amount of writing could capture her spirit, then there has been nothing which could curtail it either. Along her journey of running into red tape, she has dodged the drug lords and passed the pimps. She has side stepped the cynics and tackled the traffickers. Mam Khanyi has fronted up when many would have backed down, and as a result she has grown a galaxy of over ten thousand young stars. She loves every one of them as she has loved her own five biological children whom she has looked after on her own since her husband passed away when the youngest was a mere few months old. Every cent of her once thriving business where she made a good living for herself has been spent on making a great life for others, and nothing will stop her from continuing the work she believes she was born to do.

She gives Thanks to God, and we who meet her say Thank You too for there will always be a street child in need of love, a cup of tea, and a warm bed in her Home of Hope.

We met with Mam Khanyi twice last week, and we met with her on line. During Covid, we have missed her warm embrace and her humble story, and the reunion reignited our relationship once more. For a time, we had been stuck in the oxymoron of a virtual immersion, and our thinking had been our greatest barrier to continuing the work we love.

Mam Khanyi appeared on screen with all the same Humanity and humility which we have come to love. She engaged with the same energy and authenticity, and there was nothing virtual about our tears.

A delegate remarked that perhaps Mam Khanyi had achieved three extraordinary things with this army of orphans:

She has given them someone to love.

She has given them something to do.

She has given them something to hope for.

Mam' would reply that it was her children who gave her these gifts.

And as a few people before me have said:

"That can be enough sometimes."

P.S. Though we missed the smell of her scented candles, and the taste of her raw honey because it was a virtual meeting, what lives with us still is the warmth of her light and the sweetness of her love.

Those too, can be more than enough sometimes.

High Fives in his Heart

November in Johannesburg is a glorious month.

The weather is hot and there are the dramatic thunder showers which clear the air for some spectacular sunsets. It is also silly season which makes it glorious on the social front as well. It's a time when people start to want to do everything they've promised throughout the year but haven't gotten round to them, like early morning golf.

A bunch of us had met up at the Wanderers golf course at 6am on a Thursday morning. With plenty of moisture on the greens and no traffic at the reds, one arrives in a relaxed state. The pro shop is closed, but the caddy shack is open, and there is already an excited energy and friendly jostling for position for a bag to carry and an income to earn. Really how friendly that competition is, is something us golfers might never know. There is more than just a pleasant walk at stake here. It struck me, as it often does of how differently the golfer and the caddy have arrived at the same place. It took me 9 minutes shower door to doorman, and would have been quicker with a newer version of the VW Caravelle. I had David Grey on the CD shuttle and cool air through the conditioner as if the crisp morning air wasn't good enough. I wonder just how early Aaron had to wake up from his house in Soweto to make it to the club, or if he even has a house?

I love my golf, and there hasn't been a round in the last few years that I haven't enjoyed.

I'm still trying to learn how to enjoy every shot, but a fluffed chip or a three putt still have never made it onto the all-time cheesy grin list. From a golfing perspective this morning was no different, but I learned something else today, or maybe was just reminded of it. I've often recognised that there is a story in everyone. In some there are nursery rhymes, in others, novels. Aaron's story might easily be a tragedy but for two things. One he doesn't tell it or live it as such, and two, it is sadly more of an Everyman's tale for many of our country's people.

We were scheduled to play the nine holes before returning to work with the rest of the traffic, but I'm afraid that's a bit like dragging the half-sucked candy out of a toddler's mouth or half a beer after golf. Aaron and I soldiered on whilst the rest returned, and this is what I learned.

Aaron was born in 1961 and at the age of 2 months, suffered terrible burning from an exploding Primus stove. This left his head and face badly scarred; he also suffered the loss of two and a half fingers on his left hand, and all of his right hand. His mother ran away from the scene. Whether she was ashamed, scared, or embarrassed, he doesn't say.

He would love to be able to, if he could only find her. His search, like his life continues. His father looked after him until he was 14, and then in 1975 he too left, but as Aaron looked Heaven ward at least he knew where he went. He has no brothers and sisters. These are said matter-of-factly now, and there seems to be almost more anguish in a misread line for my birdie putt on the 13th than in his recounting of his family history.

He looks forward now, and with the same enthusiasm that he hands me the driver for the next tee shot he proudly tells me of his own family. A wife and two children—a boy of ten and a girl of nine.

"They are both at school now," he beams with an orthodontist's dream grin. He is at peace with the world and his life and he has proudly continued its circle.

"It was tough," he says, but it has made him strong. With this he rubs his calf muscle to relieve it of its most recent injury, a full-blooded three iron from under the trees which felled him like a skittle and caused him to make the point that you are not a caddy unless you've been hit. That was only this morning, yet it had only altered his style across the fairways and not his speed.

Is that all I learned? Not by a long stretch. There were stories of fate and fortune, of courage and of care, of fulfilment and fear. I also learned that it really doesn't matter where the ball goes—just imagine not being able to hit one at all.

Such different paths have brought us to the same place: The Wanderers at 6am on a November Thursday. I came from Sandton, and he came from Soweto. Me from prosperity, he from poverty.

We met at a place called Peace. He has walked these fairways for over forty years, when caddy tips were 75 cents, and bus fares were 5, and if he had his hands back, I doubt he would ever have used them to wipe a single tear of self-pity from his scarred eyes.

He has learned how to carry his handshakes in his smile and his high fives in his heart.

This much I have yet to learn; but I'm looking forward to the next lesson from this instructor of influence and example of energy.

Making Magic out of the Mundane

There was a stir in the North West corner of Ellis Park. Before any rugby test match at this iconic Highveld venue, there is always a stir, but this quarter of the stadium seemed more alive than even the sunnier and generally more raucous East stand. The crowd were on their feet and there were miniature versions of the Mexican wave going back and forth.

Every now and then a small pocket of spectators would erupt and grab at the air like flower girls collecting falling confetti, or small boys bursting balloons. There was a childlike wonderment in their antics, and it begged an answer as to why the energy here was palpably higher than in an already pumped arena.

In a scrutiny of the side-lines, where substitutes warmed up and security sauntered, there stood a cannon bombing all sorts of branded goods into the eagerly awaiting hands of the fans in the stands. Question answered. This lucky section of the field was being incentivised by manna, or in this case, merchandise from Heaven. Rugby balls both big and small were fired into the rarefied air, and the small ones would rocket into the upper echelons of the nosebleeds keeping even those higher than the Highveld ground grasping at goodies as they gasped for good gas. T-shirts that were tightly bundled up, opened like parachutes to be snatched from the sky by grateful gatherers, and few catches were dropped by the crowd.

No wonder they were having a ball. And catching them.

But hang on…

On further reflection, there were similar cannons in each corner of the field, and here there was only the odd ripple of movement as something was nonchalantly shot skywards. There just wasn't the same energised engagement as there was in the now simmering cauldron of activity in the North West.

It turned out, the secret lay not in the cannon, but in the cannon operator.

While the other three forty-five-degree compass points were sitting on their plastic chairs plopping the odd piece into the chase, North West was on his feet. With long blond shaggy hair, a t-shirt and an old pair of jeans, he would not have looked out of place on a beach with a surfboard under his arm, though he would have needed plenty of sun tan lotion to protect his lily-white skin. Running up and down the side-lines, he whipped the crowd into a frenzy, and the muzzle of the cannon moved to the momentum of the crowd.

Every freebie was a reward for crowd participation, and the conductor of this cacophony was clearly loving life in this moment. When his stock of aerial ammunition ran low, he would run a recce and grab more from the other unaware artillerymen; the crowd applauded his running like a wild hare, and when the freebies ran out, he slowly and suggestively stripped off his own shirt. He waved the t-shirt teasingly and held it aloft for a final begging before he stuffed it ceremoniously into the chute, and sent it into a cotton spinning orbit towards the loudest bidders.

He exited without a shirt but with a smile, and he left to rapturous applause—from the North West, anyway. Besides, the anthems were about to begin, but not before this skinny, longhaired showman had turned the mundane into the magical.

There are examples of this all over the place if we stop long enough to even care to take notice. The customs official who stamps hundreds of passports but who looks up and wishes you safe travels, or even better, welcome home. It might be the cashier who scans five times as much through her till in one hour as she earns in a month who smiles at your children. It is the traffic attendant who dances whilst directing traffic at a busy intersection, or the street sweeper in Cape Town who sings opera while he sweeps... And who will ever forget the washroom attendant who says with an untrainable smile, 'Welcome to my office'?

There can't be many more boring, less scenic places than a filling station bathroom; but a personally torn drying towel and a sincere smile is enough magic to make money disappear from my wallet onto his side plate.

Most people describe traffic as a prosaic and pedestrian pastime. Some time later, I was driving in the streets of Johannesburg when a billboard caught my eye. 'Smile more often', it announced.

Then another; 'Call your Mom' it advised.

Interesting. Perhaps there's a storyline developing here? Must be an advertisement for some telecoms company, I thought.

The third in the series said 'Just be Kind'—and then there was nothing.

No brand name, logo, or even a recognisable swish or slogan. I thought I'd missed the fourth poster, but I would discover in the next few days that there would be other anonymous and uplifting messages.

'Tell someone they've done a great job.'

'Treat everyone as a friend.'

Wouldn't our organisations find a free boost of support from their cultures if these simple ideas were practiced? Fractal patterns of behaviour would spiral us forward from the power stations of potential we are, to the far-flung places of possibility we could be.

There were more to follow:

'Tell someone they look great' (OK, this might be weird in some corporate settings, and no one wants a Hollywood lawsuit).

'Make someone a coffee' (We could try this in our homes too).

'Complain less. Smile more' (Imagine how much teaching would improve in our schools when heads of departments are not swamped by too many petty parental problems).

And then one which stops me in my tracks still:

'Forgive them and move on'.

This week we celebrate Mandela Day on the 18th July. He would have turned one hundred, and though his lungs may have stopped, his legacy lives on. If 785 000 people spend their 67 minutes next week in the service of others, that amounts to a shade over one hundred years of time.

For us that's a few minutes. For others it may be magnificent.

It's the least we can do.

Raise your centurion's bat Madiba, and raise it high.

You remind us still of how to make magic out of the mundane.

P.S. To: Alan Bedford-Shaw

Sarah Barrett

Bruce Copeland

Gareth Beaver

Hugh Page

Lee Foggit

And many others who have found the magic in the mundane.

Thank You, and stay magical!

Followers Change Things. Leaders Don't.

Take a deep breath. Please, I mean it.

It should be a really deep one as you need to imagine you are going under a large breaking wave. The wave and its washing machine turbulence could keep you under for a few more seconds than is comfortable. Right at this moment you have an abundant supply of oxygen in your lungs and you may even enjoy the feeling of being at the mercy of the wave as it moves your limbs where it will. You give up control for a while, your chest may start to burn a little and as you break the surface into the calm after the chaos, you suck in another huge gulp of life-giving oxygen.

But wait. Something is missing. You have done something equally important in this time to stay alive. You have done something to provide the space for the next breath.

You have exhaled.

Breathing out empties the lungs of dangerously high levels of Carbon Dioxide and clears the system for the next inhalation. It is not possible to live on the in breath alone and we need both to continue the art of living. While breathing in, the oxygen gives life. While breathing out, the absence of Carbon Dioxide sustains life.

While we lead with an inhalation, what follows is an exhalation, and we live in this extraordinary polarity eight million times in a single year. Including those moments which take our breath away.

In. Out. In. Out...Lead. Follow. Lead. Follow...

We can't have one without the other. While leadership might be the inspirational inhalation, the operational work happens in the outbreath. What leads gives life. What follows keeps you alive.

It seems out of kilter then that according to Barbara Kellerman in her book, "The End of leadership", that globally somewhere close to sixty billion dollars per annum is spent on leadership development, and perhaps zero is spent on how to be a great follower. That is akin to only taking in oxygen, and perfecting the ways of doing this. Maybe we invest in workshops on where to find better oxygen, how to master the dealings of the diaphragm and techniques for keeping the respiratory cavities clean for maximum efficiencies.

We love the idea of a purer, leading inbreath, but are we neglecting the impact of the following outbreath?

Inbreath is in. Outbreath is out. Welcome in. Keep out.

The world is littered with the hot air of great gasps of massive ideas which lie buried in the ash heap of apathy and exhaustion. Leaders who move in with promises of blue-sky breathing are left aghast as the same air gets stale and stifled in the corporate corridors of competition and is dispatched by the disengaged.

But the world is also decorated with examples of followers who have used the oxygen of ideas, handled the toxicity around them and built great relationships with their customers which have kept the company alive.

Of course, not all followers are the same as a simple exhalation. Some are passive, others show passion. Some arrive with a fully charged battery, others only with parasitic terminals searching for a charge from someone else, and perhaps part of the leaders inbreath is to see who is engaged in the uptake.

It is never the first snow flake which breaks the branch and a flood doesn't happen with a rain drop of one. It is the cumulative weight of the following rest which effects the change.

The leader says wear a mask. It is the citizens who decide whether the spread of the virus is stemmed or not.

There is a beautiful poem by Marge Piercy called *Low Road*. In it, I think she magnificently portrays the power which lies in the collective, and that collective is the life blood and the oxygen of leadership.

Low Road

What can they do
to you? Whatever they want.
They can set you up, they can
bust you, they can break
your fingers, they can
burn your brain with electricity,
blur you with drugs till you

can't walk, can't remember, they can
take your child, wall up
your lover. They can do anything
you can't stop them
from doing. How can you stop
them? Alone, you can fight,
you can refuse, you can
take what revenge you can
but they roll over you.

But two people fighting
back to back can cut through
a mob, a snake-dancing file
can break a cordon, an army
can meet an army.

Two people can keep each other
sane, can give support, conviction,
love, massage, hope, sex.
Three people are a delegation,
a committee, a wedge. With four
you can play bridge and start
an organisation. With six
you can rent a whole house,
eat pie for dinner with no
seconds, and hold a fund raising party.
A dozen make a demonstration.
A hundred fill a hall.
A thousand have solidarity and your own newsletter;
ten thousand, power and your own paper;
a hundred thousand, your own media;
ten million, your own country.

It goes on one at a time,
it starts when you care
to act, it starts when you do
it again and they said no,
it starts when you say *We*
and know you who you mean, and each
day you mean one more.

Marge Piercy

All the world's great challenges will not be solved by leaders alone. They will change when followers choose to act.

Just like the polar opposites of the two acts of breathing, we need both leadership and Followership to survive. We inhale and exhale. We lead and we follow—often in the same short breath of any slice of life.

Followers change things. Leaders don't.

I wonder if I could take in the possible and the positive, and dispel the destructive. When did I follow with all the charge in my battery and the air in my lungs? It was perhaps only at those times when anything really changed.

Breathe out...

An Influence of One

Blue light brigades are a scourge of power-hungry leaders, and remain the bane of most traffic users. A Moto GP starting grid of arrogant and over equipped motorcyclists screech up to busy intersections and shut them down while the backups build up as fast as the tempers rise. One is never sure which of their hands may be quicker to move? The flick of the wrist on the accelerator, or the hand over the arsenal of arms and glut of gadgets on the belt which must surely be the envy even of Bob the Builder. Either way you must know who is in charge.

A showroom of black SUVs usually surrounds a sleek sedan of German origin. They all have windows as dark as the paint finish of the bodywork, and the 'domestiques' close ranks around the chosen ones while they set their speed controls to cruise mode as they sail through the open intersections. As tempting as it is to wave them through with an angry arm or an avian salute, one is warned against this, as a second wave of overburdened Moto GP riders overtake the first on their way to the chequered flag of the next set of traffic lights. It is a relay race of brutal efficiency, and when the blue lights flicker away, and the sound of the sirens starts to fade, be warned again—it is still not safe to proceed.

A groupie of packed commuter taxis speed into the slipstream of opportunity like fanatics after their favourite rock star. Nature apparently abhors a vacuum, and this space after the last rider in this political peloton of power, is filled with the savvy scavengers who feed on the scraps of finite time to maximise the day's takings. I have always thought that the delegations of dignitaries should follow the taxis—they would reach their destination a lot quicker. Or better still, take taxis themselves—it would save the taxpayer much-needed millions.

Working from home has its benefits.

With this picture in my mind of the dreaded blue light brigades, I was somewhat embarrassed and a little uneasy to hear that on arrival in Accra, Ghana we would be receiving a police escort. As a facilitator with a group of executive leaders from a well- known African company, this was the accepted protocol, and so I too slipstreamed into the comfort of one of the minibuses and enjoyed the late-night trip into the Labardi Beach hotel. There was only one motorbike leading the way, and at this quiet hour on the roads, I wondered if this was at all necessary. Perhaps tomorrow and in the rush hour of an exciting and developing West African city, we would see more of a police presence?

After a world class cup of hot cocoa, a beverage we'd all fall in love with in the country of its growth, we waited dutifully and thankfully inside the air-conditioned lobby of the comfortable hotel with its colonial feel. When summonsed into the heat and humidity of the early morning, I was fully expecting to see a posse of police, yet to my amazement, their stood one. The same one who had led us from the airport a few short hours before.

Alone.

Michael Obeng Marfo is from Nsuta-mampong in the inland Sothern Ashanti region. He grew up with three sisters, one of whom, his eldest passed away. His mother looked after them all until she died in a lorry accident on the way home from a vigil on New Year's Eve 2004.

Times were tough until his uncle Eric and aunt Nelly Marfo stepped up and in his own words:

"They did what my mother could not do, and if I am a better person today, I owe it to them both."

He owes them. For he is quite simply a magnificent human being.

For our immersive groups to Ghana, he was not the blue leading light, as he hardly switched it on, but became the leading light of leadership through his example and his influence. A humble and quiet man, he adopted a confidence and a joy in his work with the metal stallion of a 900 cc Honda motorcycle beautifully under his control. With not one weapon or a Bob the Builder belt of torches or tasers, leathermans, or lasers, batons, walkie talkies, handcuffs, restraints, pepper sprays, or any other paraphernalia, he is free to move.

And move he does.

He dances through the traffic where his work and his play become one. He can change a fierce stare into a Hollywood smile in an instant and only occasionally is a finger waved in reprimand. There is a politeness in his presence and he seems to almost greet each motorist with awareness and acknowledgement. Sometimes a heel is flicked out to tell the traffic to hold their line, and every now and then, both hands come off the handle bars as he waves his arms and directs the traffic on the move. This can be done facing backwards whilst keeping his steed steady, and the traffic opens up like a new-born's lungs at birth. The passages are cleared.

I look behind to see what might fill the gap after Moses has taken his troops through the Red Sea of Accra's chaos. No one takes even a car lengths advantage. The order of disorder returns and the following army is not drowned in our wake.

The road to Tema Harbour is much like life. It has good sections and bad. It has people who help and those who hinder. There are countless distractions along the way, and sometimes there is no visible way, and a new way must be found.

On such a road one is blessed to find a guide like Michael Marfo. A man who balances the polarities of his world through both his sports and his spirituality, and above all else in the inspiration he finds in service.

The great orchestra conduct Leonard Bernstein could lead a full orchestra with just his facial expressions. Michael could lead a city's traffic with all its uncertain complexity as an influence of one.

No power or pepper spray. Just a wink, a wave and the occasional wagging finger.

And it helps to have a Hollywood smile!

A Leadership Blessing

With the food for the stomach settled, now it was food for thought

And the lessons we learn from Blessing, are gems which cannot be bought

Surrounded by Leaders who've influenced their world, Leaders who've shown us the way

To live in far brighter colours in a world depressing and grey.

We heard some harrowing stories, distressing and painful and true

And we feel the shame and the sorrow beaten both black and dark blue

This passionate Angel Blessing, she taught at a Sunday school

But she's so much more than a teacher, she stands proudly as nobody's fool.

Her time for praying was over, now it was time to act

And knowing her neighbour and all their connections became her self-driven pact

And as she did this she uncovered, a modern Pandora's box

And embarked on an activist's journey without the throwing of rocks.

She didn't bring politicians; she found a way of her own

She starts with herself, leads from behind, and nobody walks alone

Empowering others to lead, to change the plight of this place

She gathered the circles of dialogue and she gathered them all with grace.

Stop these attacks on foreigners, let's have a place where all can belong

Besides the fact it is criminal, for Humanity it's just plainly wrong

These people have skills, they have stories to tell, they can help our community grow

But if we don't let them in, we continue in sin, and well, we might never know?

I sit in this circle as a Father, and my heart feels battered and sore

As stories of my fellow Father's behaviour rock me to my very core

How will I lead and who will I impact, and how will we Dads ever learn?

That love and respect and our right to lead are just things we can only earn.

"They say in life you are judged by the legacy you left behind

But where do you go when you're frightened and how do you settle your mind?"

"Well, I have a network of love and things are not what they seem

And behind every activist woman lies her dream and a trustworthy team."

And now we have heard these stories, with all their horror and pain

And how do we live a quite different life without making mistakes again

Well, perhaps we learn here from Blessing who started by herself

And what could we do with our power within if we dusted ourselves off the shelf?

And so, she teaches these children through all possible manner and means

Without a salary or visible funding, she's lucky to feed them all beans

But yet she feeds their enquiring minds in the things they have to address

And she does it through love, and encourages poetry, and even teaches them chess.

For chess is a game of strategy which teaches a lot about life

About how to live, in uncertainty and thrive in a world of great strife

Leadership comes unexpectedly, you're never too young or too old

There may be no mine in Bhambayi, but Blessing's a nugget pure GOLD!

Steve Hall

In honour of Blessing Nyoni—a model of energy and influence, and the epitome of leadership in action.

Some Closing Questions to Keep the Conversation Open?!

We have taken a walk together along six tightropes between six different polarities, and although your balance and my balance along these continuums will be different, balance we must.

We all want better outcomes (the GET), and we know these are influenced by our behaviour (the DO). Remember though, that this was never designed to be a book about behaviour change. It was simply to allow some exploration into what the pictures (the SEE) might be which have largely driven our actions.

So, here are six questions which I have found useful in challenging my own views of the world.

- Do I open my mind to the possibility of another 'truth', and if I do, could the 'Get' be constant learning and innovation?
- Might I see the option of infinite thinking? And when I do, could it lead to more generosity and sharing?
- Could I see a friendly moment in an unfriendly situation, and will that help me build connection through relationships?

- If I saw the world as connected, rather than as separate and disconnected, how will it result in an increased ability to integrate meaning in a complex world?
- Do I really seek out, value and even celebrate uniqueness, and when I do, could I make great strides in the journey of more collaboration?
- If I want more 'fully charged' engagement, might I see that that possibility is increased when I play more with influence and energy than I do with just power and authority?

Good luck on these tightropes, and take them step by step as you lean in to a little more connection and release yourself from a world holding you in tension.

May your future have more positive Blue outcomes than challenging Red ones.

And as you walk, keep your arms out, breathe, and look up with another set of lenses.

And don't forget to enjoy the view.

Giving

Some stories are ideally told around a fire. A night time fire which lights up the faces around its warmth in the flame orange hue of its wildly licking tongues. The hiss and crackle of long pent-up air and moisture freed from the fissures in the bark are best accompanied by the call of a fiery necked nightjar in the distance as he calls for spiritual deliverance, or the whooping, haunting hysteria of a hidden hyena.

If the time is right and the audience receptive, a story, or in this case a piece of poetry finds great resonance around the energy of the bush television as people stare deeply into the burning embers of the 'hardekool' wood, and in so doing they may catch a glimpse of their own souls.

One of my favourite pieces at times like this, when energies align under a Southern Hemisphere full of scintillating stars is called 'The Cold Within', and what makes it particularly significant for me is that the author is anonymous. He or she found no need perhaps to put their name to it, sending a strong message of defiance to the ego.

THE COLD WITHIN

Six men trapped by happenstance, in bleak and bitter cold,

Each one possessed a stick of wood, or so the story's told.

Their dying fire in need of logs, the first man held his back,

For the faces 'round the fire, he noticed one was black.

The next man looking cross the way saw one not of his church,

And couldn't bring himself to give the fire his stick of birch.

The third one sat in tattered clothes; he gave his coat a hitch,

Why should his log be put to use to warm the idle rich?

The rich man just sat back and thought of the wealth he had in store,

And how to keep what he had earned from the lazy, shiftless poor.

The black man's face bespoke revenge as the fire passed from sight,

For all he saw in his stick of wood was a chance to spite the white.

The last man of this forlorn group did naught expect for gain,

Giving only to those who gave was how he played the game.

Their logs held tight in death's still hand was proof of human sin,

They didn't die from the cold without—they died from the cold within.

ANONYMOUS

If leadership is about giving, then perhaps the logs here, or the sticks of wood are the things we could so easily be giving. Time, appreciation, feedback, hope, support, care, empathy, guidance, compassion, forgiveness and even love.

Which of these precious logs of wood am I holding onto, and which harden my heart in the holding?

Whose fire might burn a little brighter if I shared the things that I can't take with me anyway when my own fire runs out?

Is this a time when the value of these things could be exponentially greater than they have ever been before?

Apart from anything else, if I gift the fire my offering, the mere act of giving will warm me both from the inside and the out. I will have been warmed twice from one simple act.

These questions still hold me curious in the tantalising tentacles of their touch as I breathe in the bushveld aroma of reflection.

In his book *12 Rules for Life*, Jordan Peterson asks a question at the end:

"What shall I do with my newfound pen of light?"

Perhaps in the same spirit I ask;

"What will you do with your stick of wood?"

I hope it will be used for warmth and light, and to keep the stories of your lives alive.

But that is your choice. And I can only wish you well along the way.

A Time to Pause

In every journey there must be time to pause.

A time to take stock, to replenish resources. To look through some old photographs and to sit around the fire while it nourishes the soul.

There is a time to stare deeply into the flames which capture the past and the future in a moment of contemplative combustion.

Perhaps, now is that time.

In Peru, on the railway trip between Cuzco and Agua Calientes, the small town just before the trek up to Machu Pichu, there is a small stop at a railway siding called Poroy. Not too much happens here, or it didn't when I was there nearly twenty years ago now, but the train stops here and while it does, window sales-folk peddle their braised corn and cheese delicacies, and a few trinkets and treasures for the tourists.

The story goes that the construction workers on this iconic railway arrived at this place. It was beautiful, they had worked hard, and someone must have said "Poroy".

"Enough for the day."

Not enough for ever, or I'm going on strike, or welcome to retirement, just "enough for now".

And so, as I reach the end of my 'second book first', I am going to say 'Poroy'.

Enough for now.

This journey has been a deeply significant one for me and as the new age dictionaries will now doubt mention, has been a "Coronacoaster" of emotions. I have reunited with some extraordinary people, ranging from Blessing, to Patrick—even in his passing. From Bongani with his newspapers and his smile to Aaron, the caddy who carries his high fives in his heart. We have met car guards and carers, taxi drivers, and waitresses who 'live in this world'. We have been tracking with Darryl, and learned the difference between chameleons and tortoises as they leave their tracks in the sand. Together we have heard from Gandhi and from car guards. We shared stories of sports and sportsmen, of elephants and Einstein, of Magicians in the mundane and of Mandela. We have eaten together and spent time at the feet of the master. We have been led through the roads of Accra by an influence of one, and shared a precious biscuit given with generosity. Together we have watched teams who have held onto belief, and listened to choirs who lift our spirits.

Maybe one theme in all these musings has been that we are always in the presence of everyday heroes, and all these heroes are already here.

This turning point along the Ziziphus branch, the 'wag-'n-bietjie,'has come full circle and it now offers us another place of possibility which lies in the presence and the story of the Leaf.

It is only at the points of most turmoil where the leaf emerges as the result of hard work, grappling with direction and tough choices.

And this leaf has three main veins.

Each one represents a key relationship in our lives.

The relationship I have with myself.

The relationship I have with others.

The relationship I have with my God, or my environment, or even something bigger.

May you find great joy in all three of those relationships.

Please visit me on www.stevehall.co.za

Here you will find all these stories and more, should you ever want to dive into a short reflection.

I will be waiting for you there.

Until then, stay safe, keep connected, and Lead with Humanity,

Poroy…'Enough for now'…

Steve Hall

ACKNOWLEDGEMENTS

There are too many people to thank, and I know I will leave a few out. Please accept my humble apologies.

To my Mom and Dad for their loving support.

To Pete Laburn for sharing with me the work I was born to do. 'May I say…'

To the Lead with Humanity team for the significance you share in that work.

To Craig Kanyemba who politely rang my doorbell and amongst other things changed my life. It is a treat having a mentor less than half my age.

To Dave Henderson and Gregg Davies and the extraordinary team at MYeBOOK for holding my hand and not letting it go.

To Lara O'Sullivan for countless hours of uploads garnished with enthusiasm.

To the countless delegates who have inspired me in classrooms, conferences and around camp fires.

To those leading cheerleaders in Annaleena, Livia, Floff, Angie, Bloss, Leigh, Peter A, Chad P, Kroggo, My Old Mate, McDuck and many others for constantly prodding me to keep writing.

To my daughter Hannah, and son Jon for giving me a million reasons to write and memories to cherish.

To my wife Cath for being the light of my life and reason for being.

To all of you who have shared a Kairos moment with me, and to all you trackers of the human spirit; I am so much richer for the time spent with you.

And lastly, to all the heroes mentioned in these pages and a multitude more who aren't, for living a life full of Humanity and always looking at that life through another set of lenses.

I read many years ago, a quote on the back of a Huletts packet of brown sugar:

"If you only have two words left to say, use them to say Thank You."

Thank You.

SUGGESTED READING AND TWO GREAT WEBSITES

Margaret Wheatley — Who do we choose to be?

Turning to one another

Finding our way

Leadership and the New Science

A Simpler way

Stephen R Covey — 7 Habits of highly effective people

First things first

Simon Sinek — The infinite game

Leaders eat last

Alex van den Heever — Changing a Leopard's Spots

& Renias Mhlongo

Boyd Varty — The Lion Tracker's Guide to Life

Ben @Rosamund Zander — The Art of Possibility

JT MacCurdy — The Structure of Morale

Abraham Twerski — Happiness and the Human spirit

Craig Kanyemba	Against All Odds
Friendly Advice	
A Motherless Child	
Alfie Kohn	No Contest
Parker J Palmer	The Courage to Teach
Ken Robinson	Finding your element
Malcolm Gladwell	Talking to strangers
Outliers	
Blink	
The Tipping Point	
Stanley McChrystal	Team of teams
Ian McCallum	Ecological Intelligence
WEBSITE 1	www.ltl.co.za
WEBSITE 2	www.leadwithhumanity.co.za

CAN I HELP?

Would you like to see more creative and innovative ideas in your team?

How about higher levels of engagement and energy at all levels throughout your organization?

Perhaps you would like to foster collaboration in your community?

What would your world look like with a better understanding of the relationships around you?

If these questions intrigue you, please visit me on www.stevehall.co.za and let's take the next steps together.

The journeys can be taken on line or face to face, in workshops, webinars, team events, immersions or conferences.

I would love to hear from you!

ABOUT THE AUTHOR

Steve Hall is a first time author with over twenty five years of experience in leadership development during the transitional years of The Rainbow Nation, South Africa. As a facilitator of learning, he has helped thousands of individuals and hundreds of teams reach higher levels of effectiveness and an increased understanding of their energy and its impact on relationships.

Steve draws on his close observations of people and their stories across communities to bring us powerful insights which surround us every day.

Steve is a lucky husband to Cath and a proud Father to Hannah and Jonathan, and is a passionate tracker, golfer and oyster diver.

Made in the USA
Las Vegas, NV
16 April 2021